# When White Is
# *Black*

by

John A. Martin, Jr.

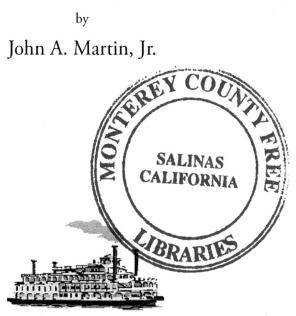

River's Bend Press

When White Is Black

First Edition

ISBN-13 978-0-9729445-4-0
ISBN-10 0-9729445-4-0

River's Bend Press
Post Office Box 606
Stillwater, Minnesota 55082 USA
www.riversbendpress.com

Edited by Jane Esbensen

The paper used in this publication meets the minimum requirements of the American National Standard for information Sciences – Permanence of Paper for printed Library Materials, ANSI Z39.48-1992

Cover design by Sential Design
www.sentialdesign.com

Library of Congress Cataloging-in-Publication Data

Martin, John A., 1931 –
    When White Is Black / by John A. Martin, Jr. – 1st ed.
        p. cm.
    ISBN-13: 978-0-9729445-4-0 (alk. paper)
    ISBN-10: 0-9729445-4-0
    1. Martin, John A., 1931 - . 2. Martin, John A., 1931 ---Family.
3. African Americans—Biography. 4. Racially mixed people—United States—Biography. 5. Racially mixed people—Race identity—United States. 6. United States—Race relations—Case studies. I. Title.
E185.97.M365A3 2005
973' .0496073'0092—dc22
   [B]                                       2005023105

*TO MY CHILDREN*

MICHAEL LAWRENCE MARTIN

CHARLES DAVID MARTIN

MARIA ROCHON NEIMAN

ALEXIS SUZANNE MARTIN

*and*

TO LLOYD AND WINONA WHOM I LOVE AND

WHO ALSO HAVE MEMORIES

# Acknowledgement

I am grateful to those who helped make this book a reality: Alison Marquess who first believed in the worthiness of the story and who painstakingly read and critiqued parts of the earliest draft of the manuscript, as did Suzanne Blackwell Alcala.

My lovely youngest daughter, Alexis Martin, patiently provided technical computer assistance, and was a major source of continuous encouragement, love and support during a period of shattering and painful change in both of our lives.

Thanks also to Mason Drukman, the biographer of former U.S. Senator Wayne Morse and a personal friend for over forty-five years, who read an early draft and offered wise counsel on how the book could be strengthened; to Lloyd Edwards, Catherine Lew, Maria and Phil Neiman, who offered sage advice; to Bill Gillohm and Bob Jones, who shared valuable family photos; to my former literary agent Claudia Menza and freelance editor, Victoria Giraud, for their assistance; and to Mary Keefe, for staunch support.

My special thanks to Richard Moran, the fine novelist and tough editor, who line-edited the manuscript and offered many invaluable rewrite suggestions.

Finally, to William Schmaltz, the publisher, and Jane Esbensen, the superb editor of River's Bend Press, my deepest appreciation for your glowing praise of *When White Is Black* and your commitment to its refinement and publication.

# FOREWORD

Fragments of this book swirled in my head and heart for many years prior to my writing it. Family and career were my life priorities and serious writing was a mere fantasy.

Nevertheless, thoughts of the impact of a mixed-race heritage on my life and the lives of past, present and future generations of my family have meandered through my mind for years like an endlessly flowing stream. I often wondered how much my own feelings of uniqueness as a person and as an African American could be attributed to how my maternal family interpreted being mulatto. At some point I realized that writing this book would help me to more clearly understand why I am who I am.

My life was greatly affected when my mother took me from my Texas birthplace to California and then suddenly and unexpectedly divorced my father. That momentous change was quickly followed by her marriage to a mixed-race African American man whose personal identity was deeply rooted in the warrior mentality of his Blackfoot Indian ancestry. These events, along with Mother's evolving drinking problem, dramatically altered the course of my life.

While a unique mixed-race background, parental divorce, my stepfather's warrior training, my intellectual father's gentleness, my stepmother's steadfast caring, and the scourge of a loving mother's alcoholism were strong motivators for writing this book, they were insufficient to bring it to fruition.

My four children and the complexity of my relationship to each of them became the final component compelling me to write *When White Is Black*. Providing my children with a family history of sorts spurred me on at the outset. Then, as I began to reflect more on my own mortality, it became increasingly important to me that my children come to truly know and appreciate me for who I am and to begin to understand the impact of the ancestral background we all share. In as many years as it took this book to gestate, it was the exact time frame it took for me to come to terms with all the reasons for writing it. What I came to discover was that this was not solely a narrative about my antecedents; it was also my story and, through me, my children's story as well. And so I dedicate this book to my children, Michael, Charlie, Maria and Alexis.

# Editorial Method

Quoted dialogue in this book is the author's creation unless otherwise attributed. This created dialogue represents my logical assumption of the exchanges which would have naturally occurred among the participants, but the words are mine and not those of the characters quoted.

In those instances in which I was a participant as listener and/or speaker, I have recreated from memory a version of the dialogue, which is as close to the actual words spoken as possible. These recreations accurately capture the essence of the thoughts, ideas and messages exchanged during those conversations. I depended heavily on family oral history in portraying characters, as well as the situations and events presented herein.

The friendship between my grandfather, Thomas Jules Peachey, and the celebrated Scott Joplin is based on the memories of my mother and grandmother, who confirmed that the two musicians had known each other in Texas.

Ed Tomkins is a fictional character, but he is based on a real defendant in a factual Houston, Texas trial of a man who was accused and convicted of a crime he did not commit. My mother was still a child when this injustice occurred, but the events so seared her mind that she later remembered critical details about the alleged crime and the unfair trial that followed.

I changed the names of certain characters to protect individual privacy. In instances where I could not track down the names of people described in my family's oral history, I invented names for them. The people my mother encountered while teaching in Orange, Texas, fall into this category.

# THE PEACHEY TREE

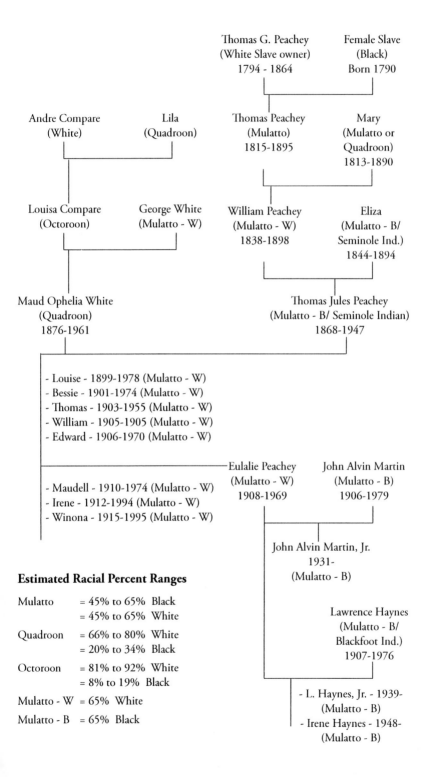

Thomas G. Peachey
(White Slave owner)
1794 - 1864

Female Slave
(Black)
Born 1790

Andre Compare
(White)

Lila
(Quadroon)

Thomas Peachey
(Mulatto)
1815-1895

Mary
(Mulatto or
Quadroon)
1813-1890

Louisa Compare
(Octoroon)

George White
(Mulatto - W)

William Peachey
(Mulatto - W)
1838-1898

Eliza
(Mulatto - B/
Seminole Ind.)
1844-1894

Maud Ophelia White
(Quadroon)
1876-1961

Thomas Jules Peachey
(Mulatto - B/ Seminole Indian)
1868-1947

- Louise - 1899-1978 (Mulatto - W)
- Bessie - 1901-1974 (Mulatto - W)
- Thomas - 1903-1955 (Mulatto - W)
- William - 1905-1905 (Mulatto - W)
- Edward - 1906-1970 (Mulatto - W)

- Maudell - 1910-1974 (Mulatto - W)
- Irene - 1912-1994 (Mulatto - W)
- Winona - 1915-1995 (Mulatto - W)

Eulalie Peachey
(Mulatto - W)
1908-1969

John Alvin Martin
(Mulatto - B)
1906-1979

John Alvin Martin, Jr.
1931-
(Mulatto - B)

Lawrence Haynes
(Mulatto - B/
Blackfoot Ind.)
1907-1976

## Estimated Racial Percent Ranges

Mulatto      = 45% to 65%  Black
             = 45% to 65%  White

Quadroon     = 66% to 80%  White
             = 20% to 34%  Black

Octoroon     = 81% to 92%  White
             = 8% to 19%   Black

Mulatto - W  = 65% White

Mulatto - B  = 65% Black

- L. Haynes, Jr. - 1939-
  (Mulatto - B)
- Irene Haynes - 1948-
  (Mulatto - B)

"Scientific scholars generally agree that there is actually no such thing as race, that mixing has been universal and perpetual and that human traits so overlap that it is impossible to describe the characteristics of one 'race' to the exclusion of all others. These scholars prefer to think in terms of a 'gene pool' that produces certain traits among inbred people more frequently than among others. What seem to be races, one might say, are actually clusters of traits."

From New People - *Miscegenation and Mulattoes in the United States*

By Joel Williamson

# EARLY ONE MORNING

The incessant ringing of the telephone jarred me out of a deep sleep. I saw the large red numbers of the clock on my bed stand through blurred eyes and I groaned. It was 3:10 a.m. I assumed the caller was my mother.

*"Damn, why does she always seem to call me so early in the morning?"* I asked the predawn darkness, despite knowing the answer as surely as I knew it was my mother, and she was probably drunk.

Over the years I had learned from experience that late night and early morning telephoning, fueled by loneliness and self-pity, is common among alcoholics. There's even a name for it. "Drink-and-dial," it's called. *Right, drink and fuckin' dial, and wake up my sorry ass.*

When I received my mother's "drink-and-dial" calls, sometimes two or three a week, her slurred greeting was usually the same. "Hullo Johnny," she'd say. "It's yurr motherr, Baby. Are ya dooin' ok?"

My answer was often a terse "fine, but tired and sleepy." On those occasions, Mother was quick to detect the irritation and disgust I managed to convey in that short, pointed response. And she would invariably fire back with whiskey-sotted sarcasm, self-pity and defensiveness.

"Well, tha's jus hunky dorie that yurr so fine. My life's not so fine and it's got nothin' t'do with drinkin', so don't you say it has."

The remainder of my mother's rambling monologue was generally the same: How intolerable it had been living with her in-laws during her brief marriage to my father, which ended thirty-eight years earlier. How she and my dad would have remained married if only they could have had a home of their own. The lingering unhappiness she'd experienced in her second marriage. And, of course, being continually and unfairly judged by her children and five sisters.

I had heard Mother's complaints so many times I could recite them flawlessly on cue. Nevertheless, I always listened to her recital of sorrows. I listened with irritation, impatience, sadness, and a monumental sense of frustration, but I did listen. Since there was no way I could stop her from drinking, I guess listening to her, no matter when she called, was the least and the most I could do.

Over the years I gradually gave in to helplessness where my mother was concerned; a bleak conviction that there was nothing I could ever do to stop her from drinking. And frankly, as a result of having a wife, three children, a career and a mortgage, my alcoholic mother was no longer among my primary concerns. Nevertheless, I answered Mother's early morning calls out of a sense of duty and, I guess, love, but with decidedly blunted compassion.

Certain, by the ungodly hour, that it was Mother calling, I placed the phone to my ear and, in a resigned monotone, said, "Yeah, I'm listening."

"May I speak with John Martin, Jr., please?" a man said.

"This is he," I answered, surprised that the voice was neither Mother's nor someone who'd dialed the wrong number.

"Hello, Mr. Martin. This is Dr. George Faulkner of the Alameda County Coroner's Office. Sorry to disturb you at this hour. I'm calling in regard to Eulalie Peachey Haynes. I understand you are Mrs. Haynes' son. Is that correct, Mr. Martin?"

*Coroner! Mother!* "Yes, I am. What's wrong?"

A wave of fear drowned my irritation, constricting my stomach, chest and throat. My wife, Jasmine, lying in the bed beside me, reached up and touched my shoulder. "Is that Mom again?" she whispered.

"It's okay, Babe. Go back to sleep," I mumbled as I slid out of bed. I walked unsteadily yet quickly into the small study adjacent to our bedroom, dragging the long telephone cable behind me.

"Mr. Martin, I'm afraid I have some bad news. Your mother was killed in a vehicular accident late last night. I'm awfully sorry to have to report such terrible news to you. And I'm doubly sorry for your loss."

For several seconds I stood beside my desk in shock, my lips moving soundlessly.

"Mr. Martin, you still there?"

"Yes, yes, I'm here," I replied, mechanically. "Are you sure it was my mother? What happened?"

"I know this is painful for you, Mr. Martin, and I am genuinely sorry for your loss. The identification is positive. Your mother was hit by a school van as she tried to cross the street in front of her apartment on Ashby Avenue in Berkeley. In all probability, she didn't see the van coming, due to the heavy rain. Apparently she stepped right in front of the oncoming vehicle. The driver never saw her prior to impact. She was pronounced dead on arrival at Herrick Hospital.

"The accident was witnessed by a friend of your mother's. She gave the police your name, and they found your telephone number in your mother's apartment. The police passed this information on to us."

"I just can't believe this. Who was the witness?"

"Let's see. Yes, here it is. A woman named Hattie Tally. She lives across the street from your mother's apartment. Ms. Tally told the police she had been drinking at your mother's place for most of the evening. When she left to go home your mother started to follow her across Ashby Avenue, and that's when the accident occurred."

I remembered Hattie. She was a neighborhood character from my teen years, a nutty-acting woman who occasionally carried on conversations with herself as she aimlessly wandered the streets of Berkeley. In those days Hattie lived with her aunt in a rooming house on Ellis Street, a few blocks from my parents' home on Harper. Little kids in the neighborhood often referred to Hattie as Bonkers Mac-Tally, or Ugly-Nutty Hattie Tattie.

I remember Mother condemned the teasing, saying, "That poor young woman is to be pitied rather than made fun of by a bunch of ignorant little brats. Besides, she's as lucid as the rest of us most of the time."

For awhile I had done as much taunting of Hattie as any kid in our neighborhood, but my mother's compassion for the woman eventually touched me and I started telling my friends to leave Hattie alone. "She can't help being crazy any more than you can help being stupid," I once told a good friend.

Now, however, with the coroner on the phone telling me Hattie Tally was the primary witness to my mother's death, I felt a surge of anger.

"You call me at three in the morning to tell me my mother's been killed in an automobile accident, and your eyewitness is a crazy person? Jesus, that woman's been a certified loony for over twenty years. She's totally unreliable. You can ask anyone who's lived in that neighborhood for awhile. They'll all tell you the woman's crazy."

"Mr. Martin, believe me, there's been no mistake here. Even if the Tally woman somehow confused some of the facts, we did recover your mother's photo I.D. and other identifying information from her apartment. However, we would still like for you to come to the morgue here in Oakland and confirm the identification."

"It's all so sudden. So hard to believe."

"I know, Mr. Martin. Tragedies like this are always hard to accept, particularly when the victim is a loved one."

"Yeah, I'm sure that's true. I guess there are arrangements I should make. Frankly, I don't know where to begin."

"Mr. Martin, let me suggest you telephone a Berkeley or Oakland mortuary. Tell the mortician that your mother is at the Alameda County Morgue, and that she will be ready for pickup after three o'clock this afternoon. The mortuary will take care of all of the details. You should, of course, confirm our identification before the mortuary comes for your mother."

"Okay, Yes, Okay. I'll come by this afternoon."

"That's fine. We'll be finished with our work by one-thirty."

"Thank you, Doctor."

"Before you hang up, Mr. Martin, there is an issue I need to clarify in order to complete the death certificate."

"Yes, what is it?"

"Your mother appears to be a white woman, but we're not one hundred percent certain, particularly given where she was living and all. What was her race, Mr. Martin?"

The coroner's perplexity momentarily tempered my shock with agitation. Even in death my mother could not avoid this central issue of her life, a question that had its genesis in generations of interracial mating, imprecise racial classification and unflagging racism.

For a moment I considered insisting on the creation of a new category on the death certificate, one accurately representing the richness and complexity of my mother's racial background. But I knew that was an utterly ridiculous thought almost as soon as it crossed my mind. How in the hell was I, a mixed-race nobody, going to change a social policy buttressed in racism and reinforced by centuries of distorted human perception in the United States?

Certainly, I could have agreed with the coroner's tentative conclusion that Mother was white. Given the limited choices available, white would have been closest to the genetic truth. But I couldn't do that either. The life my mother had lived simply would not permit me to choose that option in good faith. So I told the coroner the truth, even though I knew there was no place for that particular truth on a death certificate anywhere in the United States.

"Dr. Faulkner, my mother was sixty-five to seventy percent white. The rest of her racial gene pool was Negro and Indian. I hope that helps you," I said, knowing that Negro was the only word that would determine how he classified Mother.

"My, what an involved background. But, yes, it does give me the information I need. Thank you."

As I put down the phone, a terrible desolation overtook me. Mother was dead and she was only sixty-one. Tears welled in my eyes and I felt rotten for bitching about her early morning phone calls. For the first time since I had left the warmth of my bed, I realized that I was quite cold.

I didn't return to bed since I knew sleep at that moment was not an option. As I entered the living room, the few remaining red embers faintly glowing in the fireplace offered a suggestion of the warmth I craved. I added kindling, paper and two oak logs. The fire leaped back to life, and gradually the warm air enveloped me, although it did not penetrate the cold, deep within my soul.

I stared at the flames, thinking about the mixed-race nuances of my mother's life. She had been defined by living in a society where black was so broadly and rigidly defined that it legally and socially obliterated her physical whiteness. Was there a connection between this American racist imperative and my mother's problem drinking? This was a question I had unsuccessfully grappled with long before her death. While there may have been an indirect link, the truth was buried in the psyche of my now dead mother.

Of one thing I am certain: Mother would have been especially pleased by the coroner's confusion regarding her race. In life, she took pleasure in white people mistakenly identifying her as white, although she invariably corrected the misperception by saying, with a note of pride in her voice, that she was colored--a designation she preferred over Negro.

In a strange way the coroner's tentative conclusion that Mother was white, following what must have been a comprehensive medical examination, was a final, unofficial, affirmation of her mixed-race background.

Sadly, never during her life nor even at her death was she accorded official societal recognition of her true genetic identity. In rigidly race-conscious America, my mother was falsely classified as "Negro" only, thus enabling a white coroner to add a final, inherently racist, insult by describing her in his report as a "light skinned negress."

## Chapter 2

# Reflections

Eulalie, my mother's given name, was pronounced Eu-la-lee. Mama Peachey named Mother after a beloved family friend, an old maiden known throughout Houston's Fourth Ward neighborhoods simply as, Miss Eulalie. I don't recall anyone ever shortening Mother's name to Eula, or pronouncing it Eula-Lee, although she liked "Lee-Lee," a nickname used exclusively by her oldest niece and two of her nephews. She encouraged others to speak her name in one syllable, which tended to give it a lilting, melodic sound as it rolled off the speaker's tongue. And Mother liked that sound.

When she was a young woman, my mother was a unique beauty. Not made-up glamorous like an actress, but naturally pretty, with a bearing and attitude that complemented her good looks. She was five feet four inches tall, wore a size five shoe, and in her prime weighed one hundred and twenty pounds. Her thin lips, narrow nose, piercing dark brown eyes and wavy-curly black hair, accented her near- white, unblemished face. Her appearance suggested a Euro-Mediterranean origin to some, an unidentifiable exotic background to others. The Alameda County Coroner was only the last of many white people who understandably could not identify my mother as a Negro--the arbitrary and oversimplified American racial box to which she had been assigned.

Mother, like each of her five attractive sisters, took pleasure in her good looks. In almost all of the snapshots I remember seeing of Mother in her twenties, she presented herself in coquettish or vamp-like poses, clearly pleased with herself, and displaying immense enjoyment in being photographed.

Eulalie was proud of her white, black and Seminole Indian genealogy. She knew considerably more about her white and Indian background than she did her African roots. She told me our Caucasian ancestry on her mother's side was Parisian French, not Louisiana Cajun. The former, Mother told me, was a "purer version" of French than the latter. Once, she laughingly added, "Honey, those Louisiana Cajuns are basically "swamp folks" and French pretenders, but it really isn't nice for Mother to say that. Those poor folks are trying their best to make it, just like the rest of us."

Mother reveled in telling me how our Seminole Indian ancestors repeatedly kicked the crap out of southern whites (whom she called peckerwoods) whenever they tried to steal the Indian's Florida lands or re-enslave their adopted black kinsmen. Now that was a story I liked. It was not only action-based, like the cowboy and Indian movies I was into, but it depicted some of my relatives from long ago righteously kickin' ass, and the white man's ass at that. "Mother, please tell me again about Chief Osceola and his colored-Indian warriors," I frequently asked. After awhile, I started referring to all American Indians in a comradely way as Cuzz, - which was short for Cousin.

It was mostly within the context of her Seminole stories that my mother was also expressing pride in her African roots since, in her telling, it was always the Seminole and their adopted black brothers and sisters who beat up on the arrogant, inhumane white slavers.

I don't actually believe she possessed knowledge of a "full-blooded" African ancestor on either side of her family even though Papa Peachey, with his medium dark reddish-brown coloring, was very obviously part black. But I do know she recognized that her particular physical beauty was the result of a combining, over many generations, of European, Native American and African genealogies and, in her mind, that mixture made her regal. She often told me, "We've got practically all of it, Honey. The genes of white, red and black people intermingle in our bodies and brains, and that makes us the true royalty in this Land."

"If we're royalty, Mother," I once asked, "why ain't we rich with a lotta money?"

"Don't say ain't, Johnny, say aren't. The answer is that people who are rich with money generally get that way by stealing, or taking advantage of poor working people. We don't have any desire to steal, or to exploit others, nor does anyone in our family. So we've settled to be rich in love, spirit and dignity."

My mother also believed fervently in what she called the proper way to behave, particularly in public. I remember when I was about eight, I started riding city buses alone to attend Sunday school in Oakland. Mother instructed me to always offer my bus seat to a pregnant woman, the elderly and the infirm. "It's the polite and respectful thing to do, Johnny, and people will appreciate it, too."

Mother impressed upon me her firmly held belief that being a loudmouth in public was the height of ignorance and to be assiduously avoided. Whenever she witnessed what she considered non-circumspect public behavior by blacks she would remind me to eschew loudmouth behavior. "How you behave in public, Johnny, is a reflection on how I've raised you."

Mother taught me to pray to God daily on bended knees and to say please, thank you, and I beg your pardon, whenever appropriate. She painstakingly taught me table manners and was surprisingly patient with my miscues. When, for example, my fork or spoon made audible contact with my teeth while eating, she made no comment. She seemed to know that the dissonant sound of a silver utensil colliding with tooth enamel at the dinner table was, for me, inherently self-corrective, and she was right.

Ironically, at home, Mother was a screamer, name-caller and a door-slammer when she was angry. So I learned that it was unacceptable to be a loudmouth in public but, as a parent, you could shout obscenities at home, even if the next-door neighbors heard every word you said.

Mother almost never spanked me but, instead, complemented her screaming with threats of "backhand licks to the mouth." I told myself I would have preferred spankings and backhand licks to screaming and, when she was under the influence of alcohol, occasionally being called a "selfish little nigger ingrate," among other things. "I know one thing," I bitterly repeated to myself throughout my childhood, "When I grow up and have kids I'll never scream at 'em and call 'em bad names. Never." Later, as a parent, I did manage to successfully avoid name-calling, but, in spite of the depressing, self-loathing which followed, I periodically broke my vow against screaming.

Mother as screamer was somewhat balanced by her penchant for hugging and kissing. She was genuinely warm and demonstrative, hugging and kissing me daily until the day I decided that such mushy stuff was for younger kids.

She lovingly referred to me as "My Baby" during my boyhood, despite my stepfather's frequent reminders that her fast-growing son hadn't been a baby for some years. But I tolerated the pet name longer than I did the kisses, perhaps because it lacked the mushiness while conveying the same sense of affection.

Years before I had any serious interest in girls, Mother told me it was important that I learn to judge the character of females. She said I would avoid much grief in life if I understood that there were two basic kinds of women: good ones and bad ones. At nine years old, that sounded reasonable to me. According to Mother, sexual abstinence before marriage was the essence of goodness in girls. She always added proudly that she had been a virgin the day she married my father, two months before her twenty-second birthday.

Mother informed me that the values of sexually promiscuous girls were generally bad. They cursed, lied, cheated, stole, had poor hygiene, and sometimes even killed. They also gave boys and men venereal diseases. (It never occurred to me to ask how the bad girls got those diseases.) Then, with an audible sigh and a shake of her pretty head, I remember Mother telling me how her own brother, Tom, had contracted syphilis from a "fast little tart in Houston" when he was only a boy.

She said I should learn from my uncle's youthful misfortune and stay the hell away from girls who were fast and easy. This I did, until my hormones overcame Mother's warnings and I first experienced the delights of a woman's body.

Many of my mother's closest friends in Houston and, later, in the Bay Area, were fair-skinned mulattoes like herself, although she and her Peachey kin had darker Negro friends, as well. But I cannot recall my parents ever inviting whites to our home. Interaction with whites was part of our daily lives, but socializing with whites in our home was not. My mother and her family privately saw themselves as a proud subgroup, distinct from the black masses as well as from whites.

Mother certainly knew her brown-skinned children were vulnerable to racial hatred, but I think she also believed her degree of whiteness, and her children's to a lesser extent, was a major asset in our ongoing struggle to rise above the stultifying effects of racism. While she had definitely experienced a life in which her partial whiteness offered some relief from the anxiety, fear and danger inherent in being black in America, I never once heard my mother express a desire to live her life as a white woman, although she insisted on being accorded the same respect and dignity usually reserved for whites.

She told me many times that she believed whites, the good and bad alike, were tainted by the legacy of slavery and the bestial practice of racial bigotry. "It's a burden," she said, "I can do without."

CHAPTER 3

# MULATTO BEGINNINGS

The following observations on life in the state of
Virginia during 1778-79 are those of Thomas Anburey,
a lieutenant in the British army of General Burgoyne,
who was writing to his family in England, after being
taken prisoner during the Revolutionary War:

*Having mentioned that there are mulattoes of various tinges,
it may not be amiss to inform you from whence it arises, and no
doubt, but you will be surprised, when I tell you it is by the planters
having intercourse with their negroes, the issue of which being a
mulatto, and having connection with that shade become lighter;
as an instance, I remarked at Colonel Cole's, of whom I have made
mention; there were mulattoes of all tinges, from the first remove,
to one almost white; there were some of them young women, who
were really beautiful, being extremely well made, and with pretty
delicate features; all of which, I was informed, were the Colonel's
own. I could not help reflecting that if a man had an intercourse
with his slaves, it was shameful in the extreme, to make his own
offspring so; for these mulattoes work equally the same as those who
come from Africa. To be sure, you may say, it is a pleasant method*

*to procure slaves at a cheap rate. I imagine there could not be less than twenty or thirty mulattoes of this description, at Colonel Cole's, notwithstanding he has a very agreeable and beautiful wife, by whom he has had eight children.*[1]

Mulatto, in 17th and 18th century America, was the racial designation for a person who had a white parent and a black parent. This sufficed for awhile, but the degrees of black and white genealogy became more complex with time. Mulattoes mated with whites, other mulattoes, Indians, or blacks and additional racial labeling was necessarily invented, although it never proved adequate to account for all possible variations.

Thus, a quadroon was supposedly one-quarter black, with a white parent and a mulatto parent; an octoroon, defined as one-eighth black, was the offspring of a white and a quadroon; and a mamelouque, the child of an octoroon and a white in 19th century New Orleans, was said to be one-sixteenth black.

To simplify things for the bureaucrats, beginning with the 1850 census, all discernible white and black mixtures were called mulattoes and viewed as a separate racial category, distinct from both whites and blacks. Only in 1890 did the U.S. Census Bureau try to move beyond its black, white, and mulatto classifications by adding quadroon and octoroon categories. Census takers immediately discovered it was often impossible to visually distinguish some mulattoes from quadroons and most quadroons from octoroons.

As a result, the Bureau decided its identification of quadroon and octoroon citizens was not sufficiently accurate to justify continuing these two classifications. This decision was certainly vindicated by the later findings of anthropologist Caroline Bond Day.

---

[1]Morris Talpalar, *The Sociology of Colonial Virginia* (New York: Philosophical Library, 1960), 335-336.

In her study of over 2,500 individuals from mixed-race families over several generations, Day found that Negroes who were over half black were easily identified as black, but at the halfway point it became impossible to approximate fractions of Negro genealogy on sight, the approach used by the census takers in 1890. In her sample, Day divided mulattoes into three groups: those exhibiting more African than white characteristics, those with a balanced array of traits, and those exhibiting a preponderance of white characteristics. The latter, who Day labeled "dominant mulattoes," were almost white in appearance, sometimes even blond.

Day found that "Quadroons never combined in one person all three of the most important Negroid traits -- swarthy skin, frizzly hair, and heavy features. Octoroons were impossible to distinguish from whites." In the few octoroons she studied, she asserted, "I have been able so far to see no traces whatever of Negro admixture."

"Dominant mulattoes and 5/8 individuals (those between mulattoes and quadroons) are frequently mistaken for foreigners of various nationalities, or for white Americans, and... I know of no case of a quadroon who could not easily pass for white."[2]

From 1850 until 1920, when the Census Bureau abandoned the label, census takers commonly used mulatto to classify people with a mixture of black and white physical traits: frizzy hair and blue eyes, for instance. Of course, part of America had been white, black and mulatto ever since female African slaves began having their masters' illegitimate children a century and a half before.

Relying exclusively on the visual assessment of the census takers, the 1850 census listed 406,000 mulattoes out of a Negro population of 3,639,000. By census count alone, mulattoes in 1850 constituted 11.2

---

[2] Joel Williamson, *New People Miscegenation and Mulattoes in the U.S.* (Baton Rouge: Louisiana State University Press, 1955), 125-126.

percent of the Negro population, and 1.8 percent of the national total.[3] By 1918, the Census Bureau concluded that about three quarters of the Negro population was of mixed black and white genealogy. [4]

In spite of the Census Bureau continuing the mulatto classification until 1920, this distinct racial category never really achieved a permanent niche in the American psyche largely because Southern whites, embittered by their crushing defeat in the Civil War, channeled much of their hatred and acts of revenge toward mulattoes as much as toward blacks, doggedly insisting that the two groups were one race. This view was, of course, consistent with an implicit American racial standard which held that a single drop of "Negro blood" made one a Negro, and nothing more.

In 1930, this implicit societal racial standard became official United States policy when the Bureau of the Census issued instructions to census takers which defined the *One-drop Rule* as follows: "A person of mixed white and Negro blood should be returned as a Negro, no matter how small the percentage of Negro blood. Both black and mulatto persons are to be returned as Negroes, without distinction."[5]

Given this long history of ignorant and inflexible racial perceptions and official classifications, it is not surprising that in 1969 a white male coroner in Oakland, California looked at the cream-colored body of my dead mother and apologetically asked in veiled language whether or not she had "one drop." The affirmative answer enabled him to legally perpetuate the great American racial lie, which has habitually defined near-white people as black.

While Peachey, my mother's maiden name, has an English derivation, it is a very uncommon American surname. Identifying the first male

---

[3] *Negro Population in the U.S, 1790-1918* (Washington D.C.: U.S. Govt. Printing Office, 1918) 207-208, 210-221. For total of national population see *The Seventh Census of the United States:1850.*
[4] Joel Williamson, 125.
[5] Andrew Beveridge, *"Redefining Race,"* (New York: GothamGazette.com, Feb. 2001)

Peachey to emigrate from England to America was tantamount to uncovering the origin of my family tree.

The historical record asserts that first male immigrant as being a young man named Samuel Peachey, the eldest son of Ann Hodgskin Peachey and Robert Peachey of Milden Hall in Suffolk County, England. As a youth, Samuel, accompanied by his uncle, William Hodgskin, immigrated to America, arriving in Virginia in 1659. An article entitled "Peachey Family," published in the October 1894 edition of the *William and Mary College Quarterly* names Samuel as the first person named Peachey to arrive in America and identifies Samuel's white Peachey descendants through the late 1800s.[6]

My maternal great-great and great grandfathers, Thomas and William Peachey, had the same unique surname and favorite given names of this prominent Virginia slave holding family. Thomas, according to the 1870 U.S. Census of Galveston, Texas, was born in Virginia. The 1880 census of Galveston indicates that Thomas' son, William Peachey, was born in Florida around 1838. Both Thomas and William are described in these Galveston censuses as mulattoes.

There is strong circumstantial evidence which points to Samuel Peachey's great-great-great grandson, the white Thomas Griffin Peachey (1794-1864),[7] as the likely father of my great-great grandfather, the mulatto Thomas Peachey. The first and last names of the two Virginia born men were the same and, in 1815, the approximate year of the mulatto Thomas' birth, the family of the unmarried twenty-one-year-old Thomas Griffin Peachey owned female slaves. It certainly seems improbable that the mulatto Thomas would have had this unusual surname if he had not been biologically connected to the white Peacheys of Virginia.

---

[6] Lyon G. Tyler, Editor, *"The Peachey Family," William and Mary College Quarterly,* Vol. III, No. 2 (Williamsburg, Virginia, October, 1894), 111.
[7] Ibid, 112-115.

According to the historian Kenneth M. Stampp, "Unmarried slaveholders and the young males who grew up in slave holding families, some bearing the South's most distinguished names, played a major role in miscegenation. Given their easy access to female slaves it seems probable that miscegenation was more common among them than among the members of any other group."[8]

An additionally intriguing bit of circumstantial evidence supporting Thomas Griffin Peachey as the father of the mulatto Thomas Peachey, is contained in the U.S. Census of 1850. A Virginia census slave schedule lists Thomas Griffin Peachey as the owner of three female slaves whose ages were seventy, sixty and forty. It is not unreasonable to assume that the two older slave women had been the property of the Peachey family for many years. And in 1815, the year of the mulatto Thomas' birth, both of these women would have been of childbearing age: thirty-five and twenty-five, respectively. Either could well have been the mother of Thomas, the mulatto.

My great-great grandfather may well have been conceived in the slave quarter of the Peachey family property in Virginia. Picture a young, defenseless slave woman being repeatedly taken in lust by a man who considered her little more than a piece of property; being impregnated by him, and giving birth to his son. She names her baby after the white master who fathered him, as a reminder to the seducer and to the world of her son's birthright.

In August, 1861, Mary Boykin Chesnut, a white woman, wrote in her diary: *"I hate slavery . . . Like the patriarchs of old, our men live all in one house with their wives and their concubines, and the mulattoes one sees in every family partly resemble the white children . . . Any lady is ready to tell*

---

[8] Kenneth M. Stampp, *The Peculiar Institution: Slavery in the Ante-Bellum South* (New York: Knopf, 1956) quoted in Williamson, 53.

*you who is the father of all the mulatto children in everybody's household but her own. Those, she seems to think, drop from the clouds."* [9]

My mulatto great-great grandfather, Thomas Peachey, certainly didn't drop from the clouds. Aside from the laws of physics, his first and last names, his being mulatto, and his date and place of birth, suggest a more earthly explanation for his human presence. Still, the only tangible evidence I have of his existence and that of his wife, my great-great grandmother, Mary, is the 1870 census of Galveston, Texas, and a recording of their deaths in a family bible. This census lists Thomas' occupation as laborer and identifies Mary as a mulatto who was also born in Virginia around 1812.

Apparently, Thomas and Mary lived for a time in Florida. The 1880 census of Galveston and family oral history agree that their son William Peachey, like his future wife, Eliza, was born in Florida. Apparently, neither William nor Eliza were born into slavery.

In family oral tradition Eliza is described as a medium brown-skinned woman with long black hair and, in the eyes of the 1880 census taker, she was visibly mulatto. Eliza, whose maiden name I do not know, and her husband, William Peachey, had eight children: my grandfather Thomas, and then Mattie, William, Jr., Robert, Edward, Caroline, Oberian and Estelle, all born between 1868 and 1882.

My grandfather told me Eliza was a loving and devoted mother who was also extraordinarily protective of her children, seldom allowing them to venture too far from home. I suspect such caution reflected her sensitivity to the very real physical dangers related to living as a Negro, whether mulatto or black, in the Texas of the 1870s and '80s. But it also likely reflected my great-grandmother's deeply ingrained suspicion, fear, and distrust of white people; a legacy of her Seminole Indian heritage, no doubt.

---

[9] Mary Boykin Chestnut, *A Diary From Dixie,*(Boston: Houghton Mifflin,1949), in Williamson, 71.

Eliza's Seminole lineage is substantiated by the childhood memories of my mother and her sisters of periodic visits by government agents to their Houston, Texas home for the purpose of "registering" the eight children of their father, Thomas (Papa) Peachey, the eldest son of Eliza and William, as Seminole Indian descendants.

In addition, Joseph Banks, the grandson of Caroline Peachey, Eliza's sixth child, clearly remembers his grandmother repeatedly and proudly referring to Eliza's father as a tribal chief and warrior.

"He was a chief and he fought in the wars of the tribe before my mama was born. Yes, indeed, he was a proud chief and he fought the wars." These words of my great-aunt Caroline suggest my great-great grandfather probably engaged in the battles of the 1835-42 war the Seminole Indians fought against the United States.

According to Great Aunt Caroline, my great-great grandfather was a Choctaw tribal chief who lived in Louisiana prior to migrating to Florida, where he apparently met his daughter Eliza's mother. The 1880 Galveston census mistakenly transposed the birth states of Eliza and William Peachey's parents, listing Eliza's father and mother as Virginians and William's as being born in Louisiana and Florida.

It is likely that Eliza's father, the Choctaw tribal chief, went to Florida, like others from Southeastern tribes, with a group or band of his Choctaw clans people. Once in Florida, the Choctaw band, in accordance with prevailing custom, probably established a village with their existing leadership hierarchy intact and were thus welcomed and accepted into the ever evolving and racially mixed Seminole Alliance. And it was probably within the Seminole Nation that Eliza's Choctaw father met and wed the black or mulatto woman who later became my great-great grandmother.

The three wars between the Seminole and the United States (1817-19, 1835-42, 1855-58) were fought over the issues of land and the many runaway slaves who had been integrated into the Seminole

Nation. The goals of the U.S. Government were to re-enslave blacks and mulattoes and to remove the Seminole -- first from northern Florida, then from the entire state, for the benefit of the ever-expanding American settlement.

I cannot identify my great-great grandfather by name from the historical data currently available to me, but his daughter Eliza's 1843 birth suggests that "the wars of the tribe before my mama was born" were probably battles in the war of 1835-42. This means that my great-great grandfather was a contemporary and compatriot of Osceola (1804-1838), the best known and most celebrated of the Seminole war chiefs. It was Head War Chief Osceola, the brilliant war tactician, who epitomized the determined Indian resistance to the re-enslavement of black and mulatto Seminoles and the confiscation of the tribe's homeland by whites.[10]

Years before he earned the title of Head War Chief as a result of strategic military victories over larger and better equipped U.S. forces, Osceola's life, like the lives of many of the Indian Seminole, was deeply intertwined with his black and mulatto compatriots who had either escaped from American slavery or come to Florida as free people.

One of Osceola's two wives, Chechoter (Morning Dew), the descendant of a fugitive slave on her mother's side and of an Indian father, was herself kidnapped by whites and sold into slavery.[11] This was only one of a number of horrible incidents in his life, which led Osceola to hate whites and to steadfastly resist the kidnapping and enslavement of black and mulatto Seminoles from Florida Territory who, until 1821, were technically free citizens of Spain.

The close, indeed intimate, proximity in which Seminole of Indian, African and mixed-African descent lived encouraged sexual

---

[10] Mervin S. Garbarino, *The Seminole* (New York: Chelsea House, 1989), 47.
[11] Ibid, 49.

relations among these groups. While the Seminole lived in villages, which were sometimes based on language, tribal origin or race, these were not overly rigid demarcations. For example, James Covington notes in his book, *The Seminoles of Florida*, that Osceola's headquarters in January 1837 was located in a village occupied primarily by blacks and that his band of warriors, as late as October 1837, was composed substantially of blacks.[12]

*William Peachey*

The abolition of slavery, the defeat of the Confederacy, and the end of the Civil War resulted in the migration of mulattoes and blacks from the Northwest Territory, the Mid-Atlantic and New England states to the lower South, where the mass of uneducated, newly freed blacks were concentrated. These migrants came as missionaries, teachers and employees of the Freedmen's Bureau. Some also came as professional and business people seeking opportunity on this newly opened black frontier.

Among these latter migrants were my great-grandparents, William and Eliza Peachey, who saw New Orleans, the largest and oldest center of free mulatto life in the States, as the most opportune and exciting place

---

[12] James W. Covington, *The Seminoles of Florida* (Gainesville: University Press of Florida, 1993), 76.

to breathe the new air of universal freedom, while making a comfortable and dignified living in a business of their own. That was their dream.

Following nearly a month of search and inquiries, William found a small cafe near the French Quarter whose longtime owner had decided to sell the business and retire. The cafe was exactly what William wanted, so he struck a deal with the retiring owner.

Gradually, William and Eliza's cafe began to turn a profit and the popularity of the eatery steadily grew. William's thoughts turned to expansion of the existing establishment, and/or opening a second cafe elsewhere in the city. The year was 1868, and on March 5th of that year Eliza gave birth to a baby boy, the first of their eight children. They named the child, my future grandfather, Thomas Jules Peachey.

This was during a horrific post-reconstruction period when ominous gangs of vicious, vengeful southern white men were amassing in cities, towns and rural hamlets throughout the South. They named their terrorist organizations the Knights of the White Camellia, the Ku Klux Klan, the Constitutional Union Guards, the Pale Faces, the White Brotherhood, the Council of Safety, the White League of Louisiana, the White Line of Mississippi, and the Rifle Clubs of South Carolina. The goal of these groups was the establishment of white supremacy in every aspect of Southern life, and this meant the complete control and subjugation of all Negroes -- mulattoes as well as blacks.

These terrorist organizations publicly whipped, maimed and murdered at will. The homes and farms of Negro families were burned to the ground. Their businesses were boycotted, or broken into and physically destroyed; loans were unfairly called and property unjustly confiscated.

These terrorists came to The Peachey's Cafe in the dark of an autumn night in 1868, carrying axes and sledgehammers and, with white hoods covering their faces, they broke, pillaged and destroyed. Sturdy tables and chairs were reduced to scattered piles of splintered wood. Stoves, ovens and grills became grotesquely bent metal hulks and disengaged pieces of shrapnel. The broken glass of windows and dishes lay sprinkled like salt on a giant wound, and the pots and pans and stores of food vanished into the night in the arms of the maniacal hooded supremacists. The devastation was total.

And so it came to pass that William, Eliza and their infant son left New Orleans in 1869 and moved to Galveston, Texas, where William's parents, Thomas and Mary Peachey, were then living. William evidently continued to work in the food service business. The 1880 census of Galveston listed his occupation as "restaurateur."[13]

According to family oral history, the New Orleans experience left the four adult Peacheys shaken, anxious and bitter. It reminded them again that their social status in America was inextricably connected to that of the recently freed slaves who roamed the countryside as homeless, impoverished, despised illiterates.

It was at this time in his life that William Peachey first experienced periodic fits of depression, which he tried to combat by drinking large quantities of whiskey. But the relief which the strong drink afforded him was quite temporary, and the liquor he consumed in large quantities made him ill. He never completely gave up drinking but, after a time, he had a degree of success in moderating its use. He was helped in his struggle against excessive drinking by a combination of hard work, family and religion. Still, fits of depression periodically plagued him for the remainder of his life.

My great-great grandparents, Thomas and Mary Peachey, and their son and daughter-in-law, William and Eliza, all died in the 1890s -- Mary at age seventy-eight in 1890, Eliza at fifty-three in 1894, Thomas at

---

[13] The Bureau of the Census, *The 1880 United States Census of Galveston, Texas,* enumerated on June 12, 1880

seventy-nine or eighty in January 1895, and William in 1898 at age sixty. These deaths were recorded in a Bible owned by members of my extended family, descendants of William Peachey's eldest daughter, Mattie Peachey Thomas. The four death entries appear on the same page of the same family Bible, a copy of which I now possess.

In 1897, one year before the death of his father, William, the twenty-nine-year-old Thomas Jules Peachey married Maud Ophelia White, a twenty-one-year-old Galveston maiden, who had lived the first sixteen years of her life as a Caucasian. Together, Thomas and Maud had eight living children, one of whom was my mother, Eulalie.

## Chapter 4

## Revelation

My grandmother, Maud Ophelia White, had a mixed-race background equally as fascinating as that of her husband, Thomas Jules Peachey.

Maud's mother, my great-grandmother, Louisa Compare, was born in New Orleans around 1848. Louisa's mother, Lila, was a quadroon, the child of a white father and a mulatto mother. Louisa's father was a white Parisian Frenchman named Andre Compare. For fifteen years Lila and Andre lived together as man and wife, and Louisa was the only known child of their union.

When my great-grandmother Louisa was fourteen, her father, apparently without warning, abandoned her and her mother, Lila. In the farewell letter to his common law wife, he wrote that he had to leave the country for legal reasons. He gave no further explanation for his sudden, unexpected departure. He noted that he loved his wife and daughter, but that circumstances would not permit him to ever see them again.

Andre left seven thousand dollars in a Galveston, Texas bank account in Lila's name and pleaded with her not to attempt to locate him. He warned that it was in her and Louisa's best interest as well as his own that she not try to find him. He directed her to burn his letter and, if asked, deny that it ever existed. Finally, he suggested she wait at least two months after his departure became public knowledge, then leave New Orleans and re-settle in Galveston, or some other city.

Andre's colleagues at the New Orleans bank where he had worked as an assistant manager did not know where he had gone. He had not given any notice to the bank of his intent to leave. His friends and acquaintances also claimed not to know of his plan to leave the city, nor did they know of his whereabouts. No one seemed to know what caused his sudden departure or where he had gone. He simply vanished. Lila and Louisa never heard from Andre Compare again.

The next six years were not easy for Louisa. While she and her mother managed to live on the money Andre had left, supplemented by Lila's earnings as a seamstress, her father's desertion left her melancholy and sad. In later years she told her daughter, Maud, the story of her abandonment over and over, always with teary eyes and an anguished look, which made the young girl actually feel the pain of her mother's long ago loss. Louisa would end the story of her father's sudden and unexplained departure by suggesting he may have had a terminal illness which he hid from her and Lila, and then, to spare them the grief of seeing him die a painful death, he heroically departed.

My grandmother Maud said it probably didn't happen that way, but it made her mother feel better to believe that it did. It was more comforting than believing that Andre fled to avoid prosecution for some illegality or, worse, had had another wife and child in a faraway place, to which he decided to return.

Around 1864, Lila and Louisa moved to Galveston. Not long afterwards, Louisa met and married my great-grandfather, George White, who was a mulatto, or possibly a quadroon. What the family knows for sure is that he lived as white. On January 17, 1876, my grandmother Maud was born, the youngest of four children.

Maud White and her future husband, Thomas Jules Peachey, were said to have lived as children in the same predominately white working class Galveston neighborhood. This is not confirmed by the 1880 census, but it was not unusual for individuals, and even stable families, not to be counted by beleaguered census takers.

Unlike the William Peachey family, most of whom were brown-skinned, George and Louisa White and their children were racially indistinguishable from the white majority of their neighborhood and the city as a whole.

Indeed, the Whites went about their daily business as white people. That was how they were perceived by the outside world, and that was how they saw themselves. From family oral history, it's evident that George and Louisa were comfortable living as white, and they saw no reason to share the knowledge of their slight and distant Negro ancestries with their children.

According to my grandmother, Louisa Compare had lived her entire life on the white side of the racial divide, but my grandmother readily acknowledged knowing little of her father's background.

When Maud was a little girl, her father was an usher for Sunday services at the white First Methodist Church. My grandmother remembered him wearing white gloves and smiling with warmth and friendliness as he escorted worshipers to their seats. He touched women gently at the elbow as he guided them down the church aisle. He greeted the male worshipers with handshakes and sometimes whispered words into their ears that made them smile. As a child, it seemed to Maud that white people liked and respected her father.

George White also seemed to have good relationships with Negroes, irrespective of skin color or social status. When Maud and her father went fishing together or downtown shopping, she remembered him engaging Negroes they encountered in genuinely friendly conversations. He shook hands and talked with colored men the same way he did with whites. He even talked with them about race and how relations between Negroes and whites seemed to be getting worse rather than better, and those colored men vigorously agreed with her father on that score -- something they may not have felt comfortable doing with too many other whites.

My grandmother consistently shared memories of her childhood with her children and, early on, my mother, Eulalie, became an eager family historian. Later, Mother loved to share vignettes of family history with me. She told a story well and I thoroughly enjoyed listening to her. One of my favorites concerned a momentous episode in the lives of my great-grandfather, George White, his wife, Louisa, and their daughter, Maud.

It began one evening on the Galveston Beach when Maud was ten years old. Strolling hand in hand with her father along the beach at sunset, they were talking about her day at school and his at work when they encountered an ugly scene. Four white men were beating a colored man. The white men had knocked the colored man down and, as he lay on the sand trying to shield his face with his hands and arms, they started kicking him. George White told his daughter to stay where she was, a few yards away from the assault, and ran toward the men yelling, "y'all stop it, stop it, you gonna kill him."

Maud remembered hearing one of the men say to her father, "That's jus what we gonna do, kill this black bastard." Then another man looked at George White menacingly and said, "Are you a niggah lova, cause if you are, we gonna beat yo white ass, too."

"I ain't no nigger lover," George White responded, "in fact I hate 'em too. But there's something y'all need to know about this nigger you beatin' on."

As she listened to her father's words Maud became confused because she knew he had colored friends he liked very much.

Well, those thugs stopped beating on that colored man and they looked at George White with a mixture of curiosity and suspicion. Maud could hear the bloodied victim moaning in the sand, and then she saw him uncover his face to look at her father with beseeching eyes.

My grandmother never forgot the gist of what her father said to those awful men in an affected peckerwood drawl, and how his words degraded the colored man he was trying to save.

"That niggah y'all beatin' on is called Jeb," George White said, " and the sumbitch is a most useful niggah to very important white men over at the Port. Them men gonna be awful mad if y'all kill this niggah, 'cause they work his dumb black ass for near nothin' all day, every day, doin' work ain't fit for white men, but needs doin' jes the same. I reckon it's best for all white people that you spare him, 'cause a niggah like dis, wit so many uppity ones 'round these days, is hard to find."

All four of the thugs just stood there for a few seconds silently looking at George White while the meaning of his words penetrated their hateful minds. Finally, one of them turned to the others and signaled them to leave and they all just walked away. George got Jeb to his feet and asked him if he needed help getting home. Jeb shook his bloodied head no and staggered away from his rescuer without a word of thanks.

As Jeb walked away, Maud put her hand in her father's and pridefully looked up at his face. What she saw were tears in his eyes and, in an anguished whispery voice, he said, "I had to talk about that man that way or those hateful white trash dogs might have killed all of us."

Time passed and the ugly incident on Galveston Beach became a memory, but one Maud would never forget. She saw her father as a hero, in spite of the words he used to save Jeb's life. She tried to discuss the incident and its implications with her father as time passed, but he refused to talk about it, saying with finality that there was nothing to discuss. Finally, it became clear to Maud that the Jeb episode had had a profoundly unsettling effect on her father, so she stopped trying to get him to talk about it.

George White had a lot of friends at the Port of Galveston where he'd worked for years supervising the loading and unloading of cargoes of cotton, grain, oil and other trade goods. His co-workers would often stop by his home on a summer evening and while away the hours talking, laughing and playing dominoes on the porch. During these visits Louisa would serve fresh lemonade and sometimes join in the fun.

Maud remembered fondly that after their guests had left, her father would often tease her mother that his friends were far more impressed with her good looks and heart-shaped behind than they were with her thirst-quenching lemonade. Louisa would invariably tell George that his vivid imagination was running wild again. But he probably guessed by the lilting pitch of his wife's voice that she liked his teasingly indirect compliments, in spite of what she said.

According to my grandmother her mother was not just good-looking, but stunningly beautiful. Louisa had a smooth, unblemished, oval-shaped white face, accented by a hint of beige undertone. She also had large blue-green eyes, a small upturned nose, and long black hair with natural rose-colored highlights.

Maud didn't know what her father and his friends talked about on the front porch, because her mother wouldn't let her join them. When she asked her mother why she couldn't go out and listen, she was told that men talk about grown-up things girls don't need to hear, and wouldn't understand if they did. "Besides," Louisa would add, "your father and his friends sometimes tell each other foolish stories in language not fit for young ears."

Louisa's explanations didn't stem Maud's curiosity. She was fifteen years old then, only a few years younger than her two sisters had been when they married and left home. She thought her mother's explanations were better suited for a young child, not the young woman Maud considered herself to be at that time. So, despite her mother's admonition,

the teenaged M

and his friends

There was

and someone

conversation

a curious tee

or helping I

room easy (

outside. C

lap just in

Mau(

to men t:

boring.

cuss wo

interest in the con...

to her listening perch.

the window, she suddenly heard a voice that
with hate. The man's harsh, hurtful words
her to peek through the window. The
much older than her father and th
were white. Gradually, Maud re
her father had saved from th
Jeb was accusing Ge
and George was gentl
"That's your li
But Jeb w
the presenc
with sc
the

Remembering it decades later, Maud said she discovered a surprising enjoyment listening to the cadence and timbre of the men's voices. The integration of the different voice sounds soothed her in a way similar to the feeling she derived from barely touching the inside of one arm with the finger tips of her other hand and running the tips gently, ever so gently, up and down the arm.

One evening, as the sounds of the male voices floated through

*Maud White about 1883*

...sounded bitter and filled ...startled Maud and prompted ...speaker was an older black man, ...e two other men on the porch who ...cognized the black man as Jeb, the man ...e beating on the beach five years earlier.

...orge White of "talkin' down to him" at work, ...y denying that he had done any such thing.

...quor talking, Jeb, not you," her father said.

...s not mollified. He seemed strangely emboldened, despite ...e of the two white visitors who were suddenly looking at him ...wling faces. It wasn't customary for Negroes to talk to white men ...ay Jeb was talking to George White.

In later years, Maud said she remembered Jeb's next words as if they had been indelibly imprinted on her brain.

He said, "Troof is, yu' look an ack like yu' white, but you ain't. I know of yo' brown-skinned gramma in Port Arthur when I was a boy. She a nice woman, but her white man, yo' yella mama, yo' haf white daddy, and dat pretty white woman yu' marry don't make yu' white, so don't yu talk down to me."

The fact that my great-grandfather had "black blood" spread like an epidemic through those parts of Galveston where he and his family were known. Attitudes toward them changed overnight.

George started getting the silent treatment from the white men at the docks, and some of the whites that worked for him began to ignore his instructions. Worse still were the openly hostile bigots who tried to goad him into fights by calling him a "white nigger."

His boss didn't wait long to strip him of his supervisor's job, saying that it just wasn't proper for a colored man, no matter how fair-skinned, efficient and capable, to be supervising the work of whites. George's pay was reduced and he was reassigned to work with an all black crew of stevedores.

His new black co-workers accepted his presence among them with a restrained civility. However, they didn't go out of their way to befriend him, even though some of them knew him casually. But they were not unkind to him either, and for that George was grateful. He sensed that some of the men, particularly the mulattoes among them, silently commiserated with him. Perhaps the mulattoes were closer to being able to imagine the unimaginable -- what it must be like for a white man in America to be recast in mid-life as a nigger.

At church, most of the parishioners became aloof and decidedly less friendly toward the White family in general, and George in particular. Others began to smother Louisa with sympathy. They saw her as a tragic figure -- a white woman who had married a colored man without knowing he was colored. George resigned from his ushering position, something the white pastor made obvious he thought was only right and proper given George had suddenly changed into a colored man. Shortly thereafter, the family stopped attending services at First Methodist. For several months they didn't go to any church. Home was their sanctuary, and that was where they stayed.

Later, at the urging of their neighbors, the Peacheys, the Whites joined the African Methodist Episcopal Church. Maud and her father began attending the A.M.E. Church services sporadically at first, and then with regularity as they started to feel genuine warmth and acceptance by the pastor and members of the congregation.

Louisa attended one, maybe two A.M.E. services, but no more. She said colored folks' church services were just too emotional and demonstrative. Even the music was too loud for her. Occasional amens from the congregation punctuating points in the minister's sermon were acceptable, but when people were suddenly taken by the spirit and started shouting, dancing in the aisles and such, well, that was too much for Louisa. She said it was uncivilized behavior and that she didn't want to be in the same room while it was going on.

In addition, she felt hostility from some of the women in the church. They either refused to look at her at all, or gave her that "evil woman look," where their eyebrows pinched together so tightly that the skin bunched above their noses and their tiny bead-like eyes glowed with hate, and when she bestowed her sweetest smile upon them, they rolled their hateful eyes and looked away. Maud agreed with her mother about the mean behavior of some of the women, but she preferred to ignore the slights and, instead, allowed herself to enjoy the genuine friendliness of most of the people.

As a girl, before Jeb appeared on their porch and changed their lives forever, Maud had never thought much about her own race. She accepted the fact that she was white in the same way she accepted the reality of her two arms and two legs. She knew colored people were treated badly by many whites, but her mother and father were different. She had heard them make derogatory remarks about some blacks, but it usually had to do with what her parents considered dumb or stupid behavior, like shooting or knifing somebody because they didn't like the look on the victim's face, or behaving raucously in public.

Maud and her family had no desire to oppress black people, and they were outraged when they read about the lynching of a colored man or some other horrible mistreatment of blacks by whites. Still, if someone had asked her before her father's trouble what race she would have chosen to be if she had had a choice, she would have said white without hesitation. In fact, she would have considered the question itself downright stupid. Sweet Jesus, she was white, and in view of how colored folks were treated, there was no way she, or anyone else in their right mind, would voluntarily choose to be one of them.

Mother said that for a long while after my grandmother's sudden racial metamorphosis, Maud was consumed with thoughts related to its impact on her life and the lives of her parents. At first, the teenaged Maud felt a mixture of confusion, anger, resentment, paranoia, and fear. She couldn't understand why or how the words of an ignorant black ingrate, uttered on her family's front porch, could instantly change her life and the world around her. It made no sense to her.

Over and over she asked herself what misplaced hatred or envy or whatever it was had prompted Jeb to do what he did, particularly since her father had once saved his life. What's more, why would he and two men who were supposed to be her father's friends go around telling everybody under the sun that George White had a brown-skinned grandma? Even if her father's grandma was black as coal, why should that have anything to do with George as a co-worker, friend or neighbor? He was as white-looking as most people who call themselves white and, as far as Maud knew, he had always lived as white. What good did it do Jeb and the others to make her father and his family something they weren't?

From what my mother told me, the questions that perplexed Maud early on she was able to answer when she became aware of the pervasive nature of racism and the pain this evil inflicted upon Negroes. For the first time in her life, Maud's senses became tuned to how colored people experienced daily life, the humiliations they suffered, and the real barriers they had to overcome just to exist. Listening to what colored people had to say about their lives, she realized that even her new powers of observation missed the mountains of degradation colored people had long endured.

As for Jeb, maybe what George White said when he was saving his life offended Jeb more than being beaten up by those hateful men. In time, Maud came to believe that Jeb's betrayal fit the terrifying pattern of black men who attempt to get rid of their own self-hatred by hurting or killing other colored men. For the rest of her life, Maud remained fearful of the all too common affliction of self-hatred among colored people and its many dangerous manifestations.

While the answers derived from day-to-day life on the dark side of the American color divide helped my grandmother to begin to understand the plight of colored people, her reaction to her own immediate situation was more complex. When kids at school whispered to each other with their eyes focused on her, she immediately knew what it was about. It hurt her, but it also made her angry. And she confronted her schoolmates, all of whom she knew and none of whom she feared. She would tell them straight out she didn't appreciate being talked about and generally they sheepishly backed off.

But a larger problem for her was her tendency to see in the casual glances of strangers on the street what wasn't necessarily there. She imagined that anyone who even glanced at her silently identified her as Maud White, the girl who looked white but was really black. Sometimes she fantasized that passersby were thinking even worse things like, "that's the dirty little nigger who got away with being white for years. She ought to be taught a lesson she won't forget."

As her imagination took her deeper into darkness, she began to wonder whether some unknown whites might have plans to physically harm her or her parents. She was also obsessed with the thought that some sullen-looking black man might hold a mysterious grudge against her father and might now feel free to commit violence against him, especially since the law didn't care what you did to a colored man.

Thankfully, there were often times when she went about her daily business with race not being an issue for her at all, either in reality or in her imagination. Over time she realized that this state of grace was a luxury that flowed from her physical whiteness, and the actual experience of having lived as white.

There was something else as well, a kind of unspoken star quality which some colored people seemed to automatically bestow upon her.

When she first experienced the phenomenon it made her think of how a mediocre church choir must feel enhanced when a person with a superlative voice joins the group, and how they show their delight by making the new member feel special. Maud sometimes felt her very presence was viewed by colored folk as a gift, and she liked the feeling. She liked it very much.

Less than a month after Jeb's words changed their lives, Louisa proposed that they leave Galveston. She confessed to being terribly frightened and insisted she simply didn't possess the inner strength to live in a state of fear. She also told George that she had no intention of living the rest of her life as colored and that she was repulsed by the mere thought of doing so. Both husband and wife understood that as long as they lived together in Galveston, Louisa would automatically be considered colored by virtue of her marriage to George White.

George promised Louisa that they would move, but first he wanted to put away a nest egg to cover living expenses until he found work. That wasn't good enough for Louisa. She didn't understand why her husband couldn't go alone to New Orleans or Charleston, or even way out west to Southern California where their married daughters lived, and she and Maud could then follow after he got work.

George White was determined not to leave his family without enough money to live on during his absence. He said he would work as hard as he could and, with occasional overtime pay, they could probably save enough in six months to either leave together, or for him to leave alone and look for work.

In the meantime, George said they could begin to seriously investigate where to move by reading about other places, asking acquaintances, and even writing letters to find out where work and wages were particularly good. If they threw themselves into this kind of sensible search, George believed it would reduce some of the worry and tension their altered lives had brought them.

Maud thought it might be exciting and fun to investigate faraway places where they might live, but her mother was unimpressed. As far as my grandmother could remember, Louisa didn't even comment on her husband's idea and she didn't do any investigating.

Things didn't work out the way George White had hoped they would. He couldn't get extra hours at work, which made it very hard to save money, and Louisa grew increasingly unhappy by the day. She stopped going to the market to shop and refused to have contact with anyone other than her daughter and husband. She remained warm and loving to her child, but with her husband, George, she became withdrawn and distant, barely speaking to him when they were home together.

Suddenly, one Sunday morning, Louisa informed George she intended to take Maud and go to Brazoria, Texas to live with her mother, who had been living in that small town about fifty miles west of Galveston for a number of years. She said she planned to stay in Brazoria until George was ready to move.

My mother said she imagined my great-grandfather probably felt like a man who had been mistakenly locked in a jail cell with no way of getting out. He knew his marriage was coming apart and although he didn't want it to happen, he couldn't seem to stop it.

For the next two years, Maud spent summers and school holidays in Brazoria with her mother and lived with her father when school was in session. She slept in her father's house and prepared his meals, but much of her Galveston time was spent in the Peachey home where Eliza Peachey became like a second mother to her.

George White never left Galveston. He started drinking heavily after Louisa moved to Brazoria and Maud believed he gave up on life, although he never complained about having been reinvented as a colored man. Still, my mother reasoned, it must have been obvious to all who knew my great-grandfather that his racial metamorphosis was at the root of his problems. He was never the same confident, outgoing person he had been prior to the change and, in the end, he was a very sad, solitary man who sat in a dark corner of his house night after night drowning his pain in drink. Two years after Louisa left him, George White died of a heart attack.

Louisa remained in Brazoria where her vow never to live as colored was emphatically fulfilled. She married John Hughes, a Deputy Sheriff of Brazoria County and a distant relative of Charles Evans Hughes, an early 20th century Governor of New York, unsuccessful Republican candidate for President of the United States and, later, Chief Justice of the U.S. Supreme Court in the 1930s. My grandmother said her stepfather, Papa Johnny, was a good, kindhearted man. He was devoted to Louisa and he treated Maud like she was his very own daughter. Race was apparently not an issue in the relationship of Louisa and John Hughes, either because his background was similar to hers or his love for her transcended the *One-drop Rule*.

Over a three-year period Maud, unlike her mother, had softened to the notion of living as a colored person. In addition to feeling a certain loyalty to her father in remaining colored, she enjoyed the special status she had felt among colored folk. Not only had she developed warm and spiritually meaningful friendships among parishioners in the A.M.E. Church, she had also joined a young colored women's sewing group where the skills passed on to her by her Grandmother Lila and her mother Louisa made her an instant star. She remained very close to Eliza and William Peachey and their eight children, particularly their oldest son, Tom, whom she married in 1897.

"You know, Son," I recall my mother saying once, her eyes earnest and her hands resting gently on my shoulders, "it's fascinating how the twists and turns in the lives of our ancestors have directly affected us. You and I wouldn't have been born if my mother hadn't been turned into a colored girl, because if she had remained white, she wouldn't have married my brown-skinned father."

## CHAPTER 5

# A VERY GOOD MAN

In the summer of 1947 my grandparents, Maud (Mama) and Tom (Papa) Peachey, celebrated their fiftieth wedding anniversary. An extended family party was held one evening to honor Mama and Papa Peachey and their enduring union.

The photos of that evening depict a frail but dapper Papa Peachey in a navy blue double-breasted pinstripe suit with a white carnation in his lapel. Mama Peachey sat in a chair next to her husband's, a corsage on the right shoulder of her black dress and her lovely white hair bunched unfashionably on the top of her head. Neither smiled for the camera. Mama Peachey's face clearly projects sadness. Her husband of five decades was near death, and she knew it. Papa Peachey died on August 10, 1947, only a few weeks after his fiftieth wedding anniversary.

In the months following my grandfather's death, Mama Peachey seemed to find comfort in talking about her late husband. She particularly wanted her grandchildren to see Papa Peachey as being more than the person we in the younger generation had known -- the self-absorbed, solitary, sometimes grumpy old man, who got loaded almost daily on cheap wine or Rainier Ale and occasionally played "Danny Boy" or some other sad tune on the piano. In reality, we had hardly known Papa Peachey at all because he had spent as little time as possible around his grandchildren and, when we did see him, he had few words to say to any of us.

Mama Peachey, assisted by her daughters and sons, told her grandchildren about a Papa Peachey we never knew. I was already aware that he was a black-white-Indian man who took great pride in his mixed genealogy and steadfastly refused to see himself as exclusively black. I learned from Mama Peachey and my mother that Thomas Jules Peachey was also a good man who had lived all of his life on the margins of poverty. It's an enduring testament to his great character and heart that he sacrificed a potentially rewarding career as a musician in order to support, love, and nurture a wife and eight children, each of whom he and his wife raised to adulthood.

Tom Peachey's love of music began when he was quite young. His mother, Eliza, had what my grandmother described as "a singing voice that was a very special gift from God." Eliza sang in her church choir and young Tom often accompanied his mother to practice, where he sat enraptured by the quality of her voice. He had the ability to isolate the amazing range and deliciously pure tones of his mother's voice from what he considered the decidedly mediocre voices of the other members of the choir. During those practice sessions and on Sundays when the choir performed, Tom also listened intently to the magical sound of the piano.

One day, before the choir had fully assembled for practice, Tom left his mother's side and walked boldly to the piano. Without a word to anyone he sat down and began to play. He was nine years old and had never played a piano before. The adult choir members smiled indulgently as Tom hunched over in concentration, his face entranced as his fingers glided delicately across the ivory keys.

Miraculously, Eliza would say later, familiar notes began to emanate from the piano, faintly at first, but soon melding into a recognizable score. Conversations trailed off and heads turned to face the boy seated at the piano. As the attention of the adults focused on him, Tom, as if on cue, began to play the Lowell Mason hymn, "Nearer, My God, to Thee." He played and replayed the beginning passages, and then the middle and ending sections in turn. Finally, deftly and flawlessly, he played the entire hymn.

Eliza was stunned as the other choir members surrounded her and wondered aloud why she had kept her child's piano talent hidden. Her mouth agape, Eliza could only shake her head from side to side and insist she had no idea her son could play the piano. She swore her family had never owned a piano but, after hearing her Tom play, she told them things were likely to change. And they did.

Papa Peachey's sudden rebirth as a nine-year-old musical prodigy became one of my favorite family stories. It definitely piqued my interest and curiosity about other facets of my grandfather's life and this, of course, delighted my grandmother and my mother.

My mother told me that Papa Peachey's taste in music from the beginning was oriented toward church, light classical, marches, and other popular music of the late 19th century, including the emerging sounds of ragtime. But he and his parents despised the old "coon music," exemplified by songs like Dan Emmett's "Nigger on de Wood Pile," Stephen Foster's "Massa's in de Cold Ground," "Old Black Joe," and Ernest Hogan's "All Coons Look Alike to Me."

To the Peacheys, such music was explicitly demeaning to both black people and to themselves as mulattoes. Early on, Papa had resolved not to ever play those "nigger tunes," which he believed served to reinforce white people's racial prejudices, and colored people's identity confusion and sense of inferiority.

My grandfather's parents, according to my mother, preached a gospel of racial uniqueness to their children. It was a gospel which exalted

William's white and Eliza's Seminole Indian racial backgrounds as a way of emphasizing that they were not exclusively black, as the one drop of black blood rule would have everyone believe. They repeatedly told their children that the Southern white man's doctrine that all colored people were racially the same was a monstrous lie, which William's fair complexion and Eliza's long wavy hair dramatically underscored.

Before he was twenty, my grandfather was in demand around the Galveston area as a solo pianist at church events, social gatherings, club meetings and dances. On these occasions, he played mostly church music, marches, sentimental ballads, waltzes, polkas, and tunes from the theater. He and other local musicians also frequently came together in small bands to play at picnics and dances. Eager to make music even when a piano wasn't accessible, Papa Peachey would play the violin, banjo or drums. From the end of the 1880s through the early 1890s, my grandfather eked out a living as a musician in and around Galveston.

In the mid-1890s Papa Peachey traveled to New Orleans, the city of his birth and the place where jazz, America's only true art form, was also born. He wanted to witness firsthand this fertile music scene so close to his Galveston home. The details of Papa Peachey's New Orleans sojourn were mostly described to me by my Uncle Edward, who the family called Brother, a hard drinking, fun loving San Francisco piano bar entertainer from the late 1940s to the early 1960s.

According to Brother, Papa Peachey encountered a galaxy of musicians and bands as soon as he arrived in New Orleans. He went to see the Excelsior Band, the Indian, Columbus and the Diamond Stone bands, and many others. Music was played in the French Quarter every night, outside on the street and inside clubs. All over the city, the nights were filled with music and booze; by day, bands played at picnics and other outdoor social gatherings, including funeral processions.

The early ragtime he heard in New Orleans was not entirely new to Papa Peachey because, a few years earlier in Galveston, he had met and become friends with a fellow Texan named Scott Joplin. Joplin was later credited with being the prime creator of ragtime. In New Orleans, Papa Peachey heard various renderings of this newly evolving music. Most often it was mixed with existing forms, like minstrelsy and blues, which didn't appeal to him.

He had decided, after listening to Scott Joplin and then experimenting with the musical form himself, that ragtime should never be played fast and sounded best when the rhythm was precisely and accurately rendered. The experimental variations of ragtime he heard in New Orleans, which was sometimes played far too fast, served to reinforce his sense of how the music should not be played.

Brother told me that shortly after my grandfather arrived in New Orleans he met Achille Baquet and Dave Perkins. Baquet played clarinet and Perkins the trombone. They played with a band headed by Jack Laine, who later became one of the early white pioneers of Dixieland jazz. All of Laine's sidemen were white, except Baquet and Perkins who had blue eyes, wavy hair, light skin, and were passing for white.

Papa Peachey's father, William, could have passed for white, too. And Papa knew others who had, including his future wife and her family, until they were exposed. It is said that my grandfather had a feeling that Baquet and Perkins were "passing," even before Perkins admitted, during an evening of drinking, that he and Baquet and a whole lot of other mixed-race folks in New Orleans lived as white. What amazed Papa Peachey was that these men, when they weren't playing with Jack Laine, were frequently in the colored dives openly making music with Negroes. They brazenly passed for white when it was advantageous to do so, and then re-entered the colored world when it suited them.

Many years later, my grandfather learned that Dave Perkins and a white girl had fallen deeply in love with each other, only to part, perhaps over pressures related to race, and go their separate ways, each with a broken heart. Dave drank heavily after the breakup, became ill, and was nursed back to health by a colored woman whom he later married. The white musician's union then withdrew his union card, since his marriage to a black woman somehow ratified his being black.

It was Dave Perkins who introduced Papa Peachey to Charles "Buddy" Bolden, a blues trumpet player who is often credited by music historians with being an early bridge between blues and jazz. Papa wasn't particularly attracted to Bolden's "hot blues," which he played loudly and with a beat faster than that used in most traditional blues. Brother said that Papa liked Buddy and recognized the man as a talented musician, one of the few black musicians he had met who could read music as well as play by ear.

Buddy Bolden was very well known in New Orleans, and he knew people from all walks of life. One of his acquaintances, according to Brother, was Francine LaCour, a mulatto bordello madam who ran what was considered a classy establishment located on Basin Street. Francine catered mainly to wealthy white businessmen and politicians.

Madam LaCour needed a piano player and Buddy Bolden's new acquaintance, Tom Peachey, was a piano player in need of work. Buddy introduced Papa Peachey to Francine, noting the latter was a "social affairs business woman." The following is Brother's story of Papa's experience in Madam LaCour's establishment as he told it to me:

"Now, my papa was definitely a church boy, but he wasn't no dummy. You must believe he knew what a whorehouse was even if he'd never been in one. You also must believe that at twenty-two he'd sampled a lady or two somewhere along the way. You know he was a damn good lookin' boy in those days -- light brown-skinned, soft hair, high cheekbones, nice features, and them bedroom brown eyes. He got that dark brown-red coloring later in life from drinkin' too much cheap wine. Son, that shit'll turn you black as shoe leather if you drink enough of it, and after that, it'll kill you for sure.

"Anyway, Madam LaCour is old enough to be my papa's mama, but she was so fine, man, she busted Papa's cap. Now he didn't say that to me, but I could tell by the way he talked about her. Kept callin' her the most beautiful, classy, smart woman he had ever met in his life. The way he said in my life was a dead giveaway that my good papa'd been smitten by that Madam LaCour -- you know, the broad just blew his cap clear off!

"You know it can happen like that to any of us, Johnny," Brother told me. "A woman can capture a man's senses by the melody in her voice, the way she looks at you, her smile, the sway of her hips when she walks. It don't matter if she's a stone cold nut and can't cook a lick, some asshole man is gonna fall for her. A woman is just a powerful thing.

"Luckily for Papa, Madam LaCour wanted only a piano player, not some young googly-eyed cherry boy to keep her toes warm at night, and Papa, bein' the sensitive sort, got the message. So, Papa's first night at work, the Madam shows him the parlor where he'd be playing the piano. Soon as he enters that parlor he spots a shiny black baby grand in a corner of the room. It's the first one he'd ever seen up close and he gets real excited over the notion of playing it for Madam LaCour's socials."

I listened with rapt attention as Brother told my grandfather's story. As the story unfolded, I began to visualize the withdrawn, self-absorbed, defeated grandfather I remembered as the handsome, earnest young man Brother described. I had an overwhelming desire to know my Papa Peachey as a young man. I wanted to tell him that I was his grandson and I loved him and, because his later years would be difficult, he should live his youth to the fullest.

Brother went on. "You see, Papa was so taken by the broad's beauty and cultured manner and the fact she owned a baby grand piano, that he started believin' she was some kind of respectable society matron with the strange habit of invitin' strangers in to party every night. I guess

Buddy Bolden, who was born the same year as Papa, and Madam LaCour thought the boy had sense enough to know wit'out them spellin' it out, that he was being hired to play piano in a bordello. A classy one, but a whorehouse just the same."

At that point in the story, Brother threw back his head and laughed. And I laughed with him. It took my uncle a minute or two to regain his composure. He was enjoying his own story immensely.

"So my good papa reports to work that same night at nine. He's all decked out in his black suit, starched white shirt, and maroon bow tie. You know, Papa liked to look good, and he musta been lookin' good that night. A Negro maid opens the door and Madam LaCour meets him in the hallway.

"She's dressed in a white satin evening gown wit' a string of pearls 'round her neck and her auburn hair swept up behind and kinda piled nice and stylish on top of her head. She smiles at Papa, slips her arm in his, and escorts him to the baby grand, where she leaves him after tellin' the maid to bring him a drink. When he wasn't playin' church gigs, Papa liked to nurse a couple of bourbons straight up.

"Well, Papa sits down, forgets all about Madam LaCour, and goes right to work; didn't even take his suit coat off he's so eager to start fingerin' that baby grand. He starts out with some marches, not knowin' that people don't come to no whorehouse to hear Sousa's marches, you understand.

"Fortunately, the johns don't start comin' in 'til 'round ten, so no one objects to Papa playing marches. By the time men start filin' into the parlor Papa's workin' on show tunes, which were more appropriate to the setting. When he takes his first break and looks around, he sees about fifteen of the prettiest quadroon and octoroon girls he had ever seen together in one room.

"Most of 'em were dressed in evenin' gowns, but one or two of 'em were dressed in revealin', frilly things that looked like nightgowns. Papa had seen those kind of outfits before, but what he couldn't figure out was why some of the women were made up to look like little girls wit' big ole colored ribbons in their hair and their feet stuffed into those buckle shoes the kids wear. Even stranger, some of the other girls had on riding outfits and tall shiny boots wit' jinglin' silver spurs."

I was enjoying the humorous way Brother was telling the story, but I also didn't want it to end with my grandfather being humiliated, or worse. I guess this was a silly reaction, but for some unknown reason I felt strongly connected to this young Papa Peachey.

Brother had a crooked smile on his face as he stopped talking and I wondered whether he was fantasizing about pretty girls in shiny boots and jingling silver spurs. Whatever his thoughts, he quickly returned to the story.

"Now, sittin' at that keyboard watchin' important lookin' white men disappear upstairs with pretty, almost white, colored girls, some of 'em dressed up funny-like, Papa finally started to put two-and-two together. But Papa could be an ole ostrich bird wit' his head in the sand when he wanted to, and he wanted to then. He was so taken by Madam LaCour that he refused to accept that she ran a whorehouse. 'Course he woulda had to face the fact, baby grand or not, that he was nothin' but a piano player in a cathouse himself. Anyways, he put it out of his mind and returned to his music.

"When he played waltzes, people danced, and when he played sentimental tunes, people gathered around the piano and sang along. Papa said that while he played, the aroma in the room would gradually change. Early in the evenin' the place would smell like delicious perfume, then later like perfume mixed with cigar smoke and booze, and finally perfume mixed wit' body odors and that smell women have after sex."

"At one point that first night as he fingered the ivories, Papa felt a warm softness touch his left ear. When he turned to see what it was, he found his left eye nuzzlin' the nipple of a big sweet tittie. The way I see it, if that ole tittie had been somebody's hand and the nipple had been a dagger, it woulda been the end of Papa's left eye. Well, anyway, Papa didn't know what to do, except try to make like nothin' had happened, but he was mighty flustered. He quickly downed the bourbon remaining in his glass and turned back to the ivories. Well, the shock of that tittie in his eye made him forget what he'd been playin'."

I remember Brother again breaking into gales of laughter as he visualized scenes in the story he was telling me. And again his laughter was infectious. I laughed while visualizing my totally flustered grandfather.

"Well, the holy spirit musta taken hold of his hands 'cause Papa started playin' "Lord, I Want To Be a Christian." Right there in that house where people are doin' the nasty, ole Papa is playing "Lord, I Want To Be a Christian," and I bet he played it like his life depended on it. I don't know how long Papa kept that job at Madam LaCour's whorehouse. He never told me, and I didn't wanna make him mad by askin', but I bet it was a matter of days rather than weeks."

My mother never denied the specifics of Brother's description of Papa Peachey's adventures in New Orleans. When I asked her whether the whorehouse story was true, she said she wasn't aware of what Brother had told me.

"But, yes," she said somewhat tersely, "it's true that Papa played the piano very briefly in a New Orleans bordello." Mother quickly added, "You should bear in mind that Brother wasn't even born at the time and, as sweet as he is, he's also incapable of telling any story without adding his own exaggerated highlights."

Mother believed the most important thing to remember about Papa Peachey's New Orleans period was that he met a number of outstanding musicians, and was inspired and influenced by their music. As a result of his New Orleans experience, Papa returned to Galveston determined to organize a band of his own and eventually embark upon a career as a full-time professional musician.

In 1895, my grandfather formed the Peachey Brothers Band. It included his three brothers: nineteen-year-old Robert on mandolin, Eddie, who was twenty-one, on guitar, and twenty-four-year-old Willie on string bass. Three non-family sidemen played trombone, cornet and violin, and my grandfather played piano or drums.

*The Peachey Brothers Band Thomas Peachey sitting behind drums with his brothers Robert (mandolin), Ed (guitar), William Jr. (bass)*

Initially, the band played engagements, mostly dances, in Galveston. Later, Houston became their primary base of operation, since the work was steadier there and Papa and Mama Peachey had moved to that city following their marriage in 1897.

To Papa Peachey's dismay, the band did not make enough money to support its members and their growing families. They all had to take other jobs to survive. Undaunted, my grandfather held onto his dream of a full-time career as a musician, and for a number of years the brothers and the non-sibling sidemen continued to play the various gigs Papa managed to find.

Whenever any member of the group was unavailable for a particular engagement, my grandfather was sufficiently resourceful to fill the void with an eager, local, colored musician. Still, it became more and more apparent to Papa Peachey that joining an established and successful band or taking his own group on tour, options which required constant travel, were the only ways for him to succeed as a full-time musician. But his wife and children needed him and the support he provided, and he did not want to leave them.

Around the turn of the century, the ragtime music of Scott Joplin was starting to capture the interest of the country. Papa Peachey and Joplin had become friends in Galveston in the 1880s when Scott, who was from Texarkana, was touring the state with the Texas Medley Quartette, a vocal ensemble which included Scott, his two brothers and a neighborhood friend. The two young musicians, Tom Peachey and Scott Joplin, remained in contact through correspondence long after Scott left Texas.

Early in 1903, when the popularity of his "Maple Leaf Rag" was sweeping the nation, Scott Joplin invited Papa Peachey to come to Sedalia, Missouri and join him in a musical tour of the country. It was an unbelievable opportunity for my grandfather to achieve his lifelong dream and he knew it.

He also knew that realizing his dream was likely to create an enormous financial hardship on his family. He was worried that he might not make enough money to support his wife and children for months. And being away from them on tour would result in many difficulties for Maud, who was then pregnant with their third child. Papa had responsibilities, and shirking them was unconscionable. So he wrote to Scott Joplin and declined the invitation to come to Sedalia. He told his friend it was right and proper that he remain in Houston with his pregnant wife and two little girls, but he hoped to be able to join Joplin at a later time.

That time never came for Papa. Over the next twelve years his obligations as a husband and father steadily increased as his family grew from three to eight children. Gradually, Papa Peachey stopped playing music professionally. His musical career dreams ended, although the love of music continued to occupy a central place in his heart for the rest of his life.

"You know, JohnnyBoy," Mama Peachey once said to me while reflecting on her late husband, "your grandfather was a very good man. If he'd made music his primary focus in life instead of family, there's no tellin' what he could have accomplished. He chose family over music and worked menial jobs to support us because he loved us and it was the moral thing to do.

"Now, I know that's what God expects of all fathers, but I also know there's a lotta men who don't live up to that expectation. Those men leave their families, because they're no good to begin with, or they just crumble under the weight of responsibility. Not your grandfather, Thomas Jules Peachey. He was strong, and devoted to all of us. He was a very, very good man."

## CHAPTER 6

# NELSON STREET

My grandmother, Mama Peachey, gave birth to her first child on August 29, 1899, and her last on December 2, 1915, one month prior to her fortieth birthday. She brought nine infants into the world during that sixteen-year span; one dying just two months after his January 1905 birth.

Mama's first five infants were born in the Brazoria, Texas home of her mother and stepfather, Louisa and John "Papa Johnny" Hughes. Having her mother present during her deliveries had a calming effect on my grandmother. Since Louisa refused to set foot in the black Houston neighborhood where her daughter lived, my grandmother willingly traveled the sixty miles between Houston and Brazoria. In 1899, Mama Peachey went alone to Brazoria to give birth to Louise. On the four subsequent occasions ending in 1906, the trips to Brazoria included the Peachey children who had previously been born there--Louise, Bessie and Tom, Jr.

There is no evidence that Papa Peachey ever visited Brazoria during or immediately following any of those five births. I strongly suspect the burden of financially supporting his rapidly expanding family required that he work as much as he could. As a hotel restaurant waiter, customer tips comprised much of Papa Peachey's earnings. And most of the money he earned as a part-time musician was also derived from tips, which had to be shared with other members of the band.

There was, of course, another possible reason for Papa Peachey to stay away from Brazoria. In the late 1890s and early 1900s, people who could be physically identified as Negroes, including those of mixed ancestry like Papa, were likely to encounter genuine physical danger in small rural Texas communities like Brazoria. Mother often noted, with sadness, that hundreds and hundreds of black Americans were lynched in the United States between 1875 and 1925 -- most of them in the rural South.

My paternal grandfather, a former Houston railroad man, once told me that Brazoria County, a place of considerable Ku Klux Klan activity near the end of the 19th century, was particularly hostile to black people. How bitterly ironic that my predominately white grandmother would find love, comfort and support among her white kinfolk in Brazoria while her brown-skinned husband, the father of the babies the white Brazorians lovingly delivered and nurtured, was subject to being lynched by neighbors of his in-laws.

Born on August 28, 1908, Eulalie was Mama and Papa Peachey's sixth child and the first to be born on Nelson Street in Houston. Mother was also the first girl baby born into the family in seven years and that fact alone made her special, particularly in the eyes of her two older sisters, nine-year-old Louise and seven-year-old Bessie. Both aunts told me there was a doll-like quality about my mother, which remained with her long past infancy. Louise and Bessie also agreed that Eulalie's disposition as a child was generally mellow, although occasional fiery outbursts of anger were also part of her personality.

The rented house on Nelson Street, where Mama and Papa Peachey raised their eight children, was an old weather-beaten two-bedroom frame structure with a pitched roof. It was called a "shotgun house" because when you looked in the open front door you had an unobstructed view of the back porch. The house lacked inside plumbing and electricity. There was an outhouse in the backyard and water for drinking, cooking, washing, bathing and gardening was drawn from a faucet beside the back porch.

Mama and Papa Peachey slept in a double bed in one of the two bedrooms. Their most recent infant slept in a baby crib in one corner of their room. The girls' bedroom contained a single bed, two double beds and a small cot. The two boys slept on larger folding cots in the living room. In the stifling humid heat of the Houston summers, sleeping outside on either the front or back porch was a cooling treat for the Peachey children. Sleeping out at night offered special relief from the heat of the day, and the twinkling of the stars in the sky was endlessly fascinating.

Congested living was a way of life for the Peacheys during those years. Every morning the kids lined up one behind the other at the outhouse door. At times during the day bodies were in motion in every corner of the small house. At night the house had the feel of the inside of a sardine tin, with bodies packed tightly together on sweat-soaked mattresses.

Houston's Fourth Ward, where Nelson Street was located, consisted of a segregated pocket of black residents bordering the heart of the city. Today, the old Fourth Ward has long since been bulldozed and rebuilt as part of downtown, its former black residents scattered like ants from a ploughed-under anthill.

At the time of my mother's birth in 1908 there were no trees, lawns or sidewalks in the Fourth Ward. Since the City of Houston didn't bother to maintain the streets of the predominately black Fourth Ward, Nelson Street was continuously pockmarked with huge holes and deep ruts, which were instantly covered in ankle deep mud whenever it rained.

The Peacheys of Nelson Street were certainly poor, but all eight children were well-fed and adequately clothed. Papa Peachey's earnings from the hotel were periodically supplemented by pilfered food from the restaurant kitchen, which black cooks surreptitiously shared with him.

Later, the Houston Men's Club employed him as a porter. In both places Papa had good friends among the Negro cooks, who shared the still edible produce, fruits and meats that management had declared unfit to serve their white customers, yet refused to give to their underpaid black employees.

Clothing was Mama Peachey's domain. As a skilled seamstress she not only made clothes for the family, but she taught her daughters to sew. The older girls became adept at mending garments, which not only freed Mama to concentrate on making new clothes but also gave her time to earn money by sewing for others.

Music was a primary source of family enjoyment and fun. Papa Peachey would play the compositions of John Phillip Sousa while the children marched through the house playing imaginary instruments or pounding out the beat on their mother's pots and pans. Passers-by could also frequently hear passages from the popular tunes of the day wafting from the Peachey's living room.

Then there were the grand dances when Papa Peachey encouraged everyone, including his wife, to put on their best Sunday churchgoing clothes. Prior to this family event, Papa would have searched out clippings from magazines and newspapers picturing ballroom scenes with handsomely attired rich people dancing. Showing these to his children, he would ask them to imagine their little living room as a grand ballroom for a few hours. Each gala would begin with Papa Peachey standing beside the battered piano, impeccably dressed in his navy blue suit, sonorously announcing the names of the invitees. He would then sit at the piano and play waltzes and popular dance tunes while members of his family danced dreamily across the living room floor.

While Mama Peachey could be just as fun-loving as her husband, she was quite serious when it came to instructing her daughters in what she considered "ladylike" behavior. To my grandmother, ladylike meant the Victorian values of the 1890s, and Mama's virtue training was laden with admonitions against premarital sex.

"Why would a man buy a cow if he can get the milk for free?" my grandmother would ask her daughters, while warning them against the pitfalls and dangers of sexual relations before marriage.

Mama Peachey's virtue training went hand in hand with her firm belief that female beauty was an asset that could enable her daughters to achieve what they wanted in life. All six of the girls were pretty and their mixed-race heritage added an exotic quality to their good looks. Mama believed that her daughters' mixed-race beauty could help them to win refined, educated men who would be excellent providers, and she told them this repeatedly.

Mama also believed that a reputation for chastity enhanced a woman's natural beauty in the eyes of others. In Mama's view, most men had romanticized notions that pretty, demure females were, by definition, chaste and virginal.

"Stay out of the sun," she told her daughters. "The sun'll burn and crack your skin. Don't dye your hair 'cause dyed hair will throw your looks off kilter and can make you look cheap. And for God's sake, always dress respectably and wear colors that compliment your complexion.

"Walk with your head held high, like you're somebody. An upright bearing shows pride and dignity. You wanna carry yourself differently than no-account blacks and white trash. In this racist world we live in, you gotta show that you're different than they are. The sad reality is that your looks, bearing and color will give you half a chance in life you just wouldn't have if you were black and homely."

These were just some of the instructions for living in a racist world, which Mama Peachey instilled in her daughters, and the girls accepted and internalized their mother's rules of virtue, beauty and deportment.

The girls were also greatly influenced by the life and character of Mama's cousin Bess, whom the family called Daughter.

Daughter, who was a few years younger than Mama, lived and worked in Galveston and, by Peachey family standards, was financially well off. She even owned a stylish automobile, which she frequently drove to Houston laden with food and gifts for her cousin Maud, Papa Peachey and the children.

As a child I knew Daughter as a kind and lovely old woman with milk-white skin and sky blue eyes, which seemed to sparkle with affection when she looked at me. Her small, aquiline nose seemed to compliment her slight, shy smile. In those twilight years of her life, the childless Daughter lived in a Victorian house in Oakland with her husband Joe and a yellow tabby cat named Tess.

My mother and I often visited Daughter when I was a small boy and our soft-spoken old cousin, with an apron around her waist and an occasional vestige of flour on a hand or arm, usually had a plate of sugar cookies and a glass of milk waiting for me. Years after Daughter's death my mother told me her story.

According to my mother, Daughter's unsolicited largess to her cousin Maud's family was a major source of support for the financially strapped Peacheys. While playing in the dirt road that was Nelson Street, one or several of the children would see Daughter's car approaching and run excitedly into the house to shout the good news, "Daughter is coming! Daughter is coming!"

When Daughter visited, her automobile was generally packed with a variety of goods, including clothing, groceries, toiletries, kitchenware and sundry items. Anything she had access to and thought her cousin's family could use would be piled into her car and driven to Nelson Street. And in addition to her own purchases, Daughter also brought items to her Peachey kinfolk which had been generously donated by the women she worked with in Galveston. Even Daughter's employer, a usually unsentimental woman named Debra Arlen, was touched by her employee's devotion to her poor Houston relatives. Debra Arlen not only contributed gifts herself but also gave Daughter extra time off from her job as a whore in the thriving Galveston brothel known as Madam Arlen's.

The story of Daughter and prostitution began with the influenza deaths of her mother and father in December 1900, the same month she turned eighteen. Following her parents' deaths, the grief-stricken young woman, alone and penniless, found solace and shelter in the home of her high school Latin teacher, a white woman named Karen Morris.

Daughter and her parents, like all of Mama Peachey's relatives, had easily managed to continue living their lives as whites simply by ignoring the implications of their genetic connections to either of Mama's parents. The fact that none of the relatives lived in Galveston during the racial unveiling of Mama's father, George White, was a significant factor in their not being revealed as people with distant black ancestry who chose to live as whites in violation of the *One-drop Rule*.

Karen Morris was a once-married-and-divorced middle-aged woman who lived alone in a large house in Port Arthur, Texas, where she had taught Latin in a public high school for many years. During the time that Daughter had been a student in Miss Morris' class, the two had a very positive student-teacher relationship. Miss Morris appreciated Bess as an attentive, bright student. And like others who knew Bess, Miss Morris was also attracted to the young woman's gentle demeanor and clean good looks.

Since she had not been particularly close to Miss Morris prior to the death of her parents, Daughter was surprised and overwhelmed with gratitude when Miss Morris came to her rescue. What she did not know was that Karen Morris was not only a respected high school teacher, but also a clandestine procuress of potential prostitutes for brothels in New Orleans and Galveston. It was later learned that she made as much as $700 each for the successful delivery of vulnerable, innocent-looking young women fifteen to twenty years of age.

While caring for Bess with solicitude and motherly affection, Karen Morris offered to further help the distraught, frightened young woman obtain a good paying job. She promised to introduce Bess to a friend named Debra Arlen, whom she described as a successful Galveston businesswoman. In fact, Karen had already spoken to Miss Arlen, who said she would consider hiring young Bess as a "hostess."

According to Karen Morris, Debra Arlen's establishment catered to the most respectable men in Galveston. These clients were treated to a coterie of refined young women, all of whom Debra Arlen trained as hostesses and escorts, while caring for them as if they were her own daughters. Karen told Bess she was certain that Bess would find the work profitable and even enjoyable, if she put herself in the right frame of mind. The most important thing of all, Karen Morris told Bess, was to perform the work with skilled artistry, because this would increase her opportunities for finding and marrying a man of substance and wealth.

Emotionally vulnerable, directionless and without resources, Bess was a relatively easy mark for Karen Morris. And Debra Arlen engendered trust and a warm protectiveness, which reminded the sad young woman of her own mother, just as Karen Morris had promised. So, for a time, Daughter deluded herself into believing that hostessing, or "respectable prostitution" as Debra Arlen called it, would be her key to a happy future life. Years later, greatly influenced by cousin Maud's Peachey family, Daughter realized the truth of her exploitation.

It happened suddenly. One day Daughter began thinking about the long ago racial metamorphosis of her cousin Maud White. She had always been in awe of her older cousin's courage, and secretly ashamed of extended family members who distanced themselves from Maud because of race. One of the things Daughter had learned from prostitution was that the presumed superiority of whiteness was an evil myth and that, in the final analysis, people were simply people. She decided that day to re-establish her relationship with her cousin.

For Daughter, there was spiritual redemption in her visits to Nelson Street. She was overwhelmed by cousin Maud's unconditional love and acceptance, as well as Tom Peachey's respectful, non-judgmental attitude toward her. She was thrilled by the children's genuine affection and joy over her presence, and deeply moved by their excitement and gratitude for the gifts she brought them. Being a loving extension of the Peachey family helped Daughter to see the world differently and to regain the self-esteem she had long ago lost.

It was Daughter's relationship to Maud Peachey and Maud's family, as well as her church baptism and growing faith, which helped her to give up prostitution and eventually move to Oakland, California. There, she married a loving mulatto man named Joe Richards, who worked as a cook on the dining cars of the Southern Pacific Railroad. Daughter remained a cherished extension of the Peachey family until she died in Oakland three days before her seventy-eighth birthday.

My mother's love and compassion for Daughter was obvious to me in the sympathetic way she told the story of our old cousin. As I reflect on our visits to Daughter's home in Oakland those many years ago, I remember my mother warmly embracing the older woman. I remember the two of them sitting at the kitchen table sipping tea, talking and laughing about the old days on Nelson Street -- the love and affection the members of the family had for each other despite the cramped living, the children's excitement whenever Daughter visited, Papa Peachey's family musicals and the rigid virtue training Mama Peachey put her girls through.

And, sometimes, they discussed race. They talked about the unique mixed-race attitudes Mama and Papa Peachey passed on to their children -- the psychology, manners and culture of Mama's white-blackness, and Papa's reverence for his Seminole heritage. My mother believed the examples provided by Mama, Papa and Daughter resulted in her and her siblings having a very special appreciation and respect for themselves as mulattoes.

Over the years of my youth, Mother often spoke to me of Daughter's strength of character. I remember her saying, "That sweet, beautiful woman pulled herself out of the depths of degradation and despair to lead a good, wholesome, Christian life. I hope God has given me at least half of her courage, strength and resiliency."

## CHAPTER 7

# A BRAND OF TEXAS JUSTICE

Mr. Tomkins was the owner of a candy store on San Felipe Street, a main thoroughfare in Houston's Fourth Ward. He was a soft-spoken black man about Mama Peachey's age who had once arranged for the Peachey Brothers Band to play at a church picnic, a date so successful the band obtained several additional engagements as a result.

Mr. Tomkins and Papa Peachey became friends and occasionally had a late evening drink together in the back room of the candy store. Those nights, Mama Peachey always worried about her husband's safety because there was considerable violence on the streets of the Fourth Ward after dark, which was often ignited by the public drinking of frustrated and embittered black men.

Mama Peachey worried that her husband, with his mixed-race good looks and proud bearing, might become the innocent target of an angry, enraged Negro determined to hurt someone. The old black man named Jeb, and the irreparable damage he did to her innocent family many years earlier, had always remained in the forefront of my grandmother's memory.

Mama Peachey had nothing against Mr. Tomkins. In fact, she considered him a kind and generous man for assisting her husband and the band. She also appreciated the way he treated her children. He not only gave them sweets from time to time, but he seemed genuinely interested in their schooling.

Mr. Tomkins had this routine in which he would ask one or another of the Peachey kids to tell him about a special academic success they had had in school. If the response impressed him, he would smile, give the young scholar a small piece of candy, and remind the child that being a good student was the only road to real success in life.

"If y'all study hard'n stay in school you gonna hafa betta life den most us Negroes ever thoughta havin'," Mr. Tomkins was fond of saying.

Eulalie and Mr. Tomkins became friends when she was about nine years old. She liked the idea of earning the candy he gave her. Earning it made it taste better. Eulalie also liked the fact that Mr. Tomkins really listened to her, something she found decidedly unusual for an adult.

Mr. Tomkins wasn't like Mama Peachey, who couldn't keep still when Eulalie was talking to her and kept saying uh-huh, uh-huh in the middle of her daughter's elongated sentences. Nor was he like Papa Peachey, who usually sat in his easy chair, dozing off to the accompaniment of his own farts while Eulalie was talking to him.

When Eulalie was talking to Mr. Tomkins, he would say things like, "Is dat so," or "Well, I do declare, dat sho is interestin'." She could tell by the tone of his voice that he was truly engrossed in what she said to him. But what my mother said she enjoyed most about those long ago conversations with Mr. Tomkins was being able to fully express herself to a listening adult.

For his part, Mr. Tomkins was thoroughly impressed by how often Eulalie reported winning her classroom spelling bees. And the excellent report cards she showed him confirmed her spelling bee victories. She was not only smart and inquisitive, but she talked to him eagerly about things she had learned; the child told him of a few historical events he had known nothing about and found quite fascinating.

One series of events, which Eulalie talked about with great enthusiasm, were the Seminole Indian Wars in Florida. It thrilled Mr. Tomkins to learn that red and black men stood side-by-side, fighting whites who were trying to take the Indians' land and return the black men to slavery. Eulalie told him she was related to those proud-fighting black-red men of days gone by, a fact her father later confirmed for Mr. Tomkins.

A few months before her tenth birthday in 1918, my mother was shocked and saddened to learn from a kid at school that Mr. Tomkins' candy store was closed and its owner had been arrested for allegedly firing a pistol at a Houston policeman. She didn't believe the story at first, because the boy who told her often made up tales just to get attention. But confirmation came pretty quickly from her teacher, Mrs. Jamison, who asked everyone in class to join her in praying that no harm would come to Mr. Tomkins at the hands of the police and that he would get a fair trial in court.

My mother remembered that when Mrs. Jamison invited the class of colored children to pray with her, a boy named Billie Joe Watkins said his pappy told him "God don't come between niggers and de poleese, cause if he do, them poleese gonna know he a nigger-lova, an' God gonna get hit upside his head jus' like de niggers."

Mother said all the kids in the class roared with laughter, but Mrs. Jamison didn't crack a smile. Instead, the teacher looked at her students sternly.

My mother recalled that the look in Mrs. Jamison's eyes made her feel like she, and not Billie Joe Watkins, had made that stupid, sad statement about God, Negroes and the police. Mother said it was sad, because Negroes like Billie Joe Watkins' father were so beaten down by racism that they couldn't imagine the possibility of equality between blacks and whites.

The other kids in the class also got the message Mrs. Jamison conveyed with her eyes and they also quieted down. For several minutes, silence covered the classroom like an invisible blanket. Finally, Mrs. Jamison said, "Now we're going to pray for Mr. Tomkins' safety." And they did.

In the days that followed, my mother learned more about Mr. Tomkins' situation from her father, who had heard the story from Negroes who were at the scene on the night of the incident.

The story Papa Peachey told his wife and children went something like this: "One night after business, Ed (that's what Papa Peachey called Mr. Tomkins) was counting the day's receipts when a man came into the store, grabbed at the money Ed was counting and ran off into the night. Well, that made Ed mad, even though he wasn't sure the would-be thief had actually taken any of his money. So he picked up the gun he kept for protection and ran into the street after the man.

"He chased the fellow into a restaurant, but the man eluded him, probably escaping out the back door. As Ed left the restaurant and started to cross the street, he tripped and fell. At that time he heard a voice shout, 'Catch that nigger, he's got a gun.' The next thing poor Ed knew, he was running and two policemen were chasing him. He ran up San Felipe to Heiner and, as he turned on Heiner Street, the damn cops started shooting at him. The people who saw the whole thing said as soon as Ed heard the shots he stopped running, dropped his gun and threw up his hands in surrender.

"When the cops saw he no longer had a gun and his hands were up in the air, you would think they would have stopped shooting. Hell, they could see him as plain as day, because he was standing under a street lamp. But instead of stopping, they continued shooting, and that's how Ed got shot in the palm of his hand.

"Anyway, when that bullet hit him, Ed instinctively picked up the gun with his good hand and defended his life by shooting back at those rotten bastards. Then he ran on home and, some time later, that's where they arrested him."

According to my mother, Mama Peachey agreed with her husband that it was wrong for the police to shoot an unarmed man with his hands held high in surrender. But my grandmother also noted items from the news account Papa Peachey had failed to mention. The newspaper reporter wrote that Mr. Tomkins admitted to having had a drink or two and he couldn't describe the Negro he thought robbed him.

"I want y'all to learn from this," Mama Peachey told her children. "These white trash Houston police are no good and they'll treat Papa and the boys the same way they treat the worst acting Negro on the street. They don't see any differences among Negroes. They treat us all alike. So you got to keep your wits about you at all times."

My grandparents firmly believed that, in addition to white racism, the behavior of some Negroes also contributed to the negative social circumstances surrounding the lives of colored folks.

As much as Mama Peachey appreciated how Mr. Tomkins favored her children, she still told my mother that chasing another man up and down San Felipe Street with a gun was just plain ignorant. And chasing him with a gun after having had a few drinks, well, that was the kind of crazy Negro behavior which caused trouble and made things harder for all sensible colored folks.

Nevertheless, Mama Peachey reiterated that she believed Mr. Tomkins to be a kind and generally peaceable man who didn't intend to harm those policemen, and certainly didn't deserve to be shot by them. But Mama saved her angriest reaction to shout to Papa late one night when she thought all the children were asleep.

"For God's sake, Tom, suppose it had been one of those nights you were drinking with that fool? You coulda been hurt or put in jail, or killed for bein' in his company. You know darn well the Army killings have made white people, particularly the police, extra jumpy and trigger happy."

"Now, Maud, stop your naggin' and don't raise your voice to me," my mother heard her father reply. "You're gettin' yourself worked up for nothin'. What the hell you think I been doin' all my life but survivin' 'round darkies and white trash alike. Besides, I'm not drinkin' 'out on the street,' as you put it. Inside Ed's locked-up candy store ain't out on the street. I know the Army killings have made people jumpy, but we got to get over that and stop livin' scared. Stop worryin' and stop naggin' me, goddamit."

On it went, back and forth for an hour or more until the arguing was replaced first by the sound of my grandmother crying, and then by silence. With the silence, my mother's own tears stopped flowing, and she allowed herself to relax and join the nightly mix of rhythmic breathing from the slumbering siblings surrounding her.

What my grandparents called the Army killings were known in the media as the Houston riots of 1917. Early that year, black soldiers of the Twenty-Fourth Infantry Division had fought back against the beatings, taunts and insults of white civilians by killing seventeen of their tormentors. Following what historian John Hope Franklin called "a pretense of a trial,"[14] thirteen Negro soldiers were hanged for murder and mutiny, forty-one were imprisoned for life, and forty others were held for further investigation. Negroes across the United States were outraged at what they considered a blatant miscarriage of justice.

A black newspaper in Baltimore editorialized, "The Negroes of the entire country will regard the thirteen Negro soldiers of the Twenty-Fourth Infantry executed as martyrs," and an article in the "New York Age", another Negro paper, stated, "Strict justice has been done, but full

---

[14] John Hope Franklin, *From Slavery To Freedom,* third edition (New York: Knopf, 1967), 406.

justice has not been done . . . And so sure as there is a God in heaven, at some time and in some way, full justice will be done."[15]

One year after the Houston riots, Ed Tomkins was indicted by a grand jury for assault with a deadly weapon with intent to commit murder. It is not unlikely that a traumatized black community saw Mr. Tomkins' indictment as an extension of the injustice perpetrated in Houston twelve months earlier.

During the two-day trial, Eulalie sat with Mrs. Jamison and five other students from her all-Negro school, in the segregated, colored section at the rear of the courtroom. Mrs. Jamison had obtained permission from Dr. Rhodes, the school principal, to select six students from various grades to attend the trial of Ed Tomkins as a special civics project. The six students were required to write essays and participate in school forums on the court proceedings and the criminal justice system.

The only spectators in the courtroom were the children, Mrs. Jamison, members of Mr. Tomkins' family, two rows of curious colored people, and the witnesses who were called to testify. As a result of the sparse attendance, the children's view of the proceedings over the unoccupied rows of seats reserved for whites was unimpeded.

Mr. Tomkins was tried before an all-white jury, people who were patently not his peers. He sat very erect at the defense table, and Eulalie would occasionally catch a glimpse of his bandaged hand. She also saw his white, court-appointed attorney, who Mrs. Jamison said hadn't done very good lawyering for colored folks in the past.

"Why," Eulalie wondered aloud, "does Mr. Tomkins have the man as his lawyer if he isn't a good lawyer?"

Mrs. Jamison lowered her head and whispered that people who didn't have money to pay for a real good lawyer had to settle for one appointed by the court.

---

[15] Ibid

Eulalie thought the policeman who shot Mr. Tomkins was a handsome looking man in his dark blue uniform and shiny black shoes. He was tall and thin, like her father's brother, Uncle Eddie, and he had big green eyes and wavy brown hair like her mother's Brazoria cousins, Cliff and Lawrence. In fact, he looked quite a bit like Cousin Lawrence, she thought, so much so that she wondered if he could be related.

When asked under cross-examination to explain how Mr. Tomkins could have sustained a bullet wound in the palm of his shooting hand if he was firing his revolver, Officer Reiner's face suddenly reddened. But, instead of answering the question, he pointed his finger at Mr. Tomkins and shouted, "That niggah sittin' there wit his niggah self called me a white son-of-a-bitch, shot at me and tried to kill me. That niggah sittin' there in front of y'all tried to kill me."

Eulalie, whose attention had drifted from the trial to thoughts of Daughter's upcoming visit to Nelson Street, immediately refocused on her surroundings as she heard the policeman shout his accusation. The hatred in his voice not only jolted her out of her reverie, but it also frightened her. She was afraid for Mr. Tomkins, and she wondered why the judge did not scold the policeman for calling Mr. Tomkins a nigger.

My mother told me it was at that point in the trial that she suddenly didn't want to be in that courtroom. She felt fear she didn't understand and had never before experienced. It was as if the air in the courtroom had thickened with the poisonous breath of hate and the sweaty stench of lifelong victimization. She began to wonder whether the vile atmosphere she sensed in the courtroom could even change her into something mean and ugly.

She wanted to be at home with her family, where the evils of the outside world could not penetrate. But her ten-year-old heart reminded her that Mr. Tomkins was her friend, and remaining in court would honor their friendship. So she stayed, and the anxiety lessened, but it never entirely left her.

Mr. Tomkins told his story to the jury pretty much the way Papa Peachey had described it to his family. Later, my mother learned from Mrs. Jamison that three eyewitnesses, who were prepared to corroborate Mr. Tomkins' version of the events, were never called to testify.

After the trial, the defense attorney said he didn't consider the eyewitnesses to be entirely credible, so he didn't call upon them to testify. But the three people told a Negro newspaper reporter that neither the police, district attorney, defense attorney, nor anyone else for that matter, ever asked them to testify about what they had seen that night.

When the defense concluded its case, the presiding judge, whom my mother remembered as a very fat, balding man with long, gray sideburns, gave instructions to the jury, which included definitions of assault and murder.

Later, in language all of the children could understand, my mother said Mrs. Jamison explained assault as someone trying to physically hurt or injure another person, no matter what weapon was used or how badly the victim was hurt. Murder, she explained, was one person intending to and then killing another person. But if one person is trying to kill another and the second person kills the first while defending himself, then it isn't murder, but self-defense.

The judge's instructions to the all-white jury were, of course, grievously flawed by the double racial standard, which defined the criminal justice system throughout the state of Texas. For example, he made no mention of the right to defend one's self against assault with a deadly weapon. Nor did he make clear that, even if the policeman had been killed, the most Mr. Tomkins could be found guilty of was manslaughter.

Even if he had been convicted of manslaughter, which the children learned was a lesser crime than murder, the fact that Mr. Tomkins had never committed a felony should have resulted in his receiving probation instead of going to jail. Since neither Officer Reiner nor his partner was killed, the only possible charge against Ed Tomkins should have been assault and battery. With the help of a local Negro attorney, Mrs. Jamison painstakingly explained the judge's omissions to the children, once they were back in the classroom.

"But why," Eulalie had wanted to know, "did the judge forget to tell the jury about self-defense?"

No one said anything. The other children just looked at Eulalie like she was the dumbest thing on the face of the earth not to know it was because of race. My mother said she ignored both the silence and the looks and, instead, said to her teacher, "We should go tell the judge right now that he forgot to tell them about self-defense. Please, Mrs. Jamison, he'll listen to you, I know he will."

Mother told me she'd never forget what happened next. Mrs. Jamison started crying and suddenly embraced her. Mother said the teacher's arms engulfed her whole head.

"It was like she was shielding me from a barrage of stones being thrown by a mob I couldn't see," Mother remembered. "It simply never occurred to me that Mr. Tomkins wouldn't get a fair trial because he was black. Even after that policeman screamed nigger and the judge ignored it, even as shocked and afraid as I was, I nevertheless believed that the courtroom was a place of fairness for everyone."

The all-white jury in the Tomkins case evidently saw one issue--a black man shooting a gun at a white policeman. They found Ed Tomkins guilty of assault with intent to commit murder. The judge unhesitatingly handed down the harshest penalty available to him. He sentenced Ed Tomkins to confinement in the State penitentiary for ten years.

My mother told me she broke down and cried when the judge passed sentence, while two burly cops swiftly handcuffed the piteous candy storeowner and ushered him out of the courtroom. She cried not only for Mr. Tomkins, but also for the injustice her youthful mind told her had been done that day. She found no comfort in the words of a Negro she overheard saying, "He lucky he ain't dead, 'cause if he didn't have his gun, dem crackers woulda shot his black ass to pieces."

Following the trial, my mother experienced what she later realized was a state of depression. She moped around the house and, for the first time in her life, hid under her bed on several occasions so she could be completely alone. She was easily brought to tears over the bickering of siblings, something she normally handled with aplomb. Worst of all, for some time after the trial she was haunted by the possibility that her very own father could be subjected to the kind of injustice that had taken Mr. Tomkins away from his family.

Later, as her sadness sank beneath daily layers of childhood experiences, my mother told herself that Papa Peachey was probably a little safer than Mr. Tomkins because he wasn't as black as Mr. Tomkins. She knew that she and her family were clearly different, and that others must surely see the difference as well.

Indeed, the United States Censuses of 1910 and 1920[16] identified the Peacheys of Nelson Street as mulattoes. Had the family been around during the experimental 1890 census, a sharp-eyed enumerator may have identified Mama Peachey as octoroon, or quadroon, Papa as mulatto, and the children as mulattoes and/or quadroons. While the Peachey family clung tenaciously to these distinctions, in the real world the *One-drop Rule* meant that whites considered them to be no different than the blackest Negro in America.

---

[16] Bureau of the Census, *Fourteenth Census of the United States: 1920 Population, Houston, Texas, January 14, 1920.*

## CHAPTER 8

# TEACHING SCHOOL AT EIGHTEEN

Following her 1926 graduation from Booker T. Washington High School in Houston, Texas, my mother was hired to teach Negro children and youth in a ramshackle, one-room schoolhouse in Orange, Texas. Orange is a small deep-water port city on the Sabine River and the Gulf Intra-coastal Waterway, located about 100 miles east of Houston.

While Eulalie had achieved an excellent academic record and was highly recommended for the Orange job by her high school principal and teachers, she was, nevertheless, ill prepared for the awesome challenge which confronted her. She was only eighteen years old and had not received any formal training in teaching or in classroom management. Nor had she had the benefit of serving an apprenticeship under an experienced teacher.

Eulalie did have the counsel of her older sister, Louise, who had taught in the same Orange school six years earlier. Louise was also remembered favorably by many of the Negro residents of Orange, and it was she who had arranged for her younger sister to live with The Reverend and Mrs. Dewey and their two children.

Reverend Dewey was the pastor of the Orange Hope Baptist Church, which was attended by many of the community's black residents. My mother considered herself fortunate to be living with the Deweys since it gave her added legitimacy within the black community. In the beginning she was anxious and even a little fearful about her safety, but being a member of the Dewey's household helped to lessen her fears. Most importantly, Mrs. Dewey turned out to be a wise, understanding and supportive surrogate mother to the eighteen-year-old girl living away from home for the first time in her life.

My mother described the schoolroom in Orange where she taught as "simply primitive." She said there were places in the unfinished wooden walls where sunshine streamed through the cracks. She remembered the room contained about twenty battered seats with attached desks. The students sat in rows facing the front of the room, where a large blackboard, in surprisingly good condition, covered most of the wall behind the teacher's table and chair.

Her students ranged in age from six to seventeen and several of the bigger teenagers could not comfortably fit their long legs under the desks. These youngsters were forced to sit at an angle with their feet and legs in the aisle.

In the rear of the room stood a large, wood-burning stove and on both sides of the stove were single wooden chairs without desks. I remember my mother shaking her head sadly and saying, "You know, those ole red neck crackers in Orange had plenty of money in the city and county coffers to improve Negro schools. They were just too ignorant, mean and hateful to do it."

Eulalie was understandably nervous as she faced her first day on the job. Her youth, inexperience, and lack of training weighed heavily upon her. A number of the students towered over her five foot four inch frame, including a sullen, muscular teenager named Dooley Sims, who leered menacingly at the cute little fair-skinned teacher.

To make matters shockingly worse, an enormous dummy ambled into the room with the regular students on the first day of class. No one had informed Eulalie that a six foot, two hundred pound, twenty-two-year-old imbecile man named Lester would be joining the twelve girls and eight boys who were officially assigned to her class.

Later that first day, the school principal explained that Lester's family had moved to Orange from Beaumont three years earlier. He was considered harmless, and hadn't caused problems for Eulalie's predecessor. The racially segregated State of Texas didn't provide special educational services for retarded Negroes like Lester. Out of compassion and as a convenience to his working parents, the Negro school administration permitted Lester to attend their school. The principal assured his young teacher that Lester wouldn't be a serious distraction but, if he became one, the school would discontinue allowing him in her class.

Mother said she cried herself to sleep that first night, then had a nightmare in which she was trapped in a dark room with a leering Dooley and an expressionless Lester slowly advancing toward her. She screamed hysterically as Dooley's hands gripped her shoulders.

She awoke, drenched in perspiration, to the gentle voice of Mrs. Dewey saying, "It's alright, child, wake-up, wake-up, now. You been havin' a bad dream. Just screamin' your pretty head off. What's wrong, honey?"

Eulalie told Mrs. Dewey about the dream and about her day at school. She described how Dooley had looked at her lasciviously the entire day and how she hadn't expected anything like Lester. She suddenly wasn't sure she was up to this job. She told Mrs. Dewey that she wanted to go home.

My mother remembered how Mrs. Dewey cradled her shoulders and rocked her back and forth while talking in a soothing, comforting voice. She told my mother that Lester was a gentle, obedient soul who wouldn't cause her trouble. As for the Sims boy, Mrs. Dewey initially expressed surprise that my mother at eighteen hadn't gotten used to boys like Dooley reacting to her in that way.

Mrs. Dewey explained to my mother that, unfortunately, there were a great many colored boys like Dooley Sims. They were angry, resentful and hateful toward anyone who wasn't as black and beaten down as they felt themselves to be. They felt powerless to strike back at white people. But let them get near fair-skinned colored people and their resentments come out in a torrent.

Still holding Eulalie in her arms, Mrs. Dewey said that every black man in the South knows that merely looking at a white woman can cost him his life and this bitter reality twists the minds of some black men so badly that they start believing they can find self-esteem by possessing a near-white woman's body.

My mother said she'd had a prior sense of what Mrs. Dewey said that night about black men because her mother had talked to her in a similar way. And she had certainly experienced seething resentment of her whiteness from darker skinned Negro peers. But those experiences didn't help to lessen the anxiety she'd felt being in that small room all day long with Dooley Sims.

Mother said Mrs. Dewey was a very persuasive woman that night as she argued that the Dooley Sims' problem could be overcome by uncovering the goodness in him with dedicated teaching. And she said my mother had to also show Dooley that she wasn't afraid of him.

"Honey," my mother said she remembered Mrs. Dewey saying, "you got this whole Negro community behind you. If Dooley Sims laid a finger on you, he would be in a heap of trouble and he knows it, too."

In addition to assuring my mother that she had widespread community support and protection against potential physical harm, Mrs. Dewey told her she must sincerely want to help even her most difficult students to learn, and she must project that desire to every child in her class.

"You know," my mother said, "that kindly woman talked to me for at least two hours that night. She was so wise and caring that I felt ashamed I'd wanted to quit and run home to my mama."

The day after Eulalie's nightmare, Mrs. Dewey organized a group of women from her husband's church to walk my mother to and from school each day. That escort service helped to relieve my mother's anxiety, and it also gave her additional opportunities to talk to the parents of her students.

A typical school day with the eighteen-year-old Eulalie as teacher involved a lot of recitation, memorizing, silent reading, practice writing, and doing arithmetic problems on the blackboard. She felt one of the biggest hurdles she faced was not being able to teach all of her students at the same time due to their different grade levels. She taught reading, grammar, spelling, writing, arithmetic, geography and history, and had to stagger instruction in each subject to accommodate four learning levels. There was simply no way to resolve this problem in her ill equipped one-room schoolhouse in Orange, Texas.

"Lord knows I did my best, but you know, Johnny, teaching all those subjects in one room to kids of different ages and grades, while trying to keep discipline too, kept me so busy that I didn't have time to think of more interesting ways to teach. My emphasis was primarily on recitation and memorization. Even in history, for the most part, I didn't have time to talk about the lives of people. Instead, I usually had those kids memorizing names and dates, names and dates, over and over. I've always loved history and it broke my heart to have to make it so dry and dull, but for most of the year I felt I just didn't have time to do anything else."

My mother said she generally organized her teaching day into morning and afternoon sessions. In the morning she had her students doing reading, spelling, grammar and arithmetic and, in the afternoon, reading, history, geography and writing. She remembered that she made liberal use of the blackboard throughout the day.

Just as Mrs. Dewey had predicted, Lester turned out to be less of a distraction than Mother had feared. Before he left home each day, Lester's mother instructed him not to be disruptive in class. He was to sit quietly in his chair and mind the teacher. If he had to go to the bathroom, he was to raise his hand, but that was the only time he was permitted to raise his hand. And, of course, he must obey the teacher at all times. If he didn't obey Miss Peachey, he would no longer be permitted to attend school.

As it turned out, Lester was the best-behaved student in the class. Every day he entered the room and quietly took his seat in one of the chairs on either side of the stove in the rear of the room.

My mother always greeted him with a warm smile and a friendly, "Good Morning, Lester."

Lester would respond with a wide grin, a nod of his head and a loud, "Mornin', Miz Peach," which invariably produced giggles from his classmates.

Although he wasn't issued books like the regular students, an undaunted Lester brought his own book from home. It was his mother's cookbook. Later, Eulalie borrowed picture magazines from the Deweys and other families, which she brought to school for Lester to leaf through while the other students were engaged in learning. The magazines evidently delighted Lester. He told "Miz Peach" he liked the pictures and he studied them with an enviable intensity. When students were doing reading exercises, Lester would open the cookbook or a magazine, making sure to turn a page whenever he heard a reader do so.

My mother said that while she and Lester got along famously from the outset, tension remained between Dooley Sims and herself. He was surly and withdrawn. He continued to look at her in what she considered a sexually suggestive way, although his actual behavior toward her was not inappropriate. Nevertheless, she continued to feel uneasy in Dooley's presence for weeks.

In spite of her fears, Eulalie tried hard to treat Dooley fairly. She quickly learned that he was considerably behind others his age. His reading level was so low that it astounded her. One of her seven-year-old students, a girl named Willa Mae, had reading skills superior to Dooley's. He could add a short column of single numbers, but that was the best he could do in arithmetic. The only states he could name were Texas, Louisiana and Mississippi. The only President of the United States whose name was familiar to him was Abraham Lincoln. While she began to understand part of the reason for his attitude, she continued to remain uneasy in his presence.

One Saturday morning as Eulalie was returning to the Dewey residence following a trip to the neighborhood grocery store, she saw Dooley and another of her teenaged students, Eddie Lee Turner, standing beside a tree, engaged in heated conversation. Mother said her first impulse was to reverse course and return to the grocery store in the hope the boys would not see her. But suddenly, Dooley hit Eddie Lee in the face with his fist and quickly followed up with a flurry of punches, knocking Eddie Lee to the ground.

"Johnny," my mother said, "to this day I don't know what got into me. I just ran to those boys, yelling at Dooley to stop hitting Eddie Lee."

Mother said Dooley was evidently so surprised to see her and to hear her yelling at him that he "just stood there at first lookin' stupid, but it didn't take him long to try to intimidate me with his evil glare.

"You know what, Johnny? I just glared right back at his black ass and I walked right up to his face and told him not to lay another hand on Eddie Lee. Then I asked him why he wanted to hurt his friend. At first he refused to answer so I kept askin', and finally he lowered his head, looked down at the ground and told me why he punched Eddie Lee."

Eulalie learned that a few of the older kids in her class, including Eddie Lee, had been calling Dooley dumb and teasing him because he was in a reading group with little kids. Dooley told his teacher he wasn't coming back to school and he was gonna beat the stuffin' outta anybody in that school who said bad things about him.

Mother told me her momentary reaction to Dooley's intent to quit school was elation. Good riddance, she thought. There will be less tension in my life with that evil nigger gone from my classroom. But just as quickly as that feeling of relief surfaced, it was replaced by the imagined voices of her mother, sister Louise and Mrs. Dewey. Those loving voices said that helping Dooley was her responsibility and that meant trying to keep him in school and teaching him as best she could.

In the next instant the eighteen-year-old teacher reached up and touched Dooley Sims on his shoulder. "Raise your head and look at me, Dooley," she commanded.

Slowly the boy raised his head and looked into his teacher's face. Eulalie saw tears welling in his eyes. For the very first time she sensed the personal degradation and pain of the sullen boy she had feared every day for so many weeks. And in the emotion of that moment, Eulalie struggled to retain her own composure.

She heard herself telling Dooley she cared about him, as did others, and she sincerely wanted him to remain in school. She promised to try to make school a much better place for him if only he would give her another chance.

Dooley looked away from his teacher's face, but she knew he was listening. When she asked him a second time to give her and school another chance, Dooley turned and faced his teacher again. There was no meanness in his mirthless look, but there was a hint of hope. He nodded yes, then turned without speaking and walked away from his young teacher.

The first thing Eulalie did when school resumed the following Monday was to place Dooley in a different reading group. No longer would he be required to read with the younger children. After asking the school's principal for advice, Eulalie decided to create a new group composed of mostly older students with differing reading skills. Members of the new group read from one of three books, each of which reflected a different level of difficulty.

The move into the new reading group had almost an instant impact on Dooley Sims. His sour mood sweetened, his surliness disappeared and he became less withdrawn.

Encouraged by Dooley's improved attitude, Eulalie began to involve him in deciding how many pages he should read each day. Away from the hearing of the other students she would ask questions like, "Dooley, do you think six pages is about right or do you think you can handle a few more?"

Dooley clearly appreciated the sensitivity and caring which characterized the new relationship he had with his teacher. He began saying "Yes, Ma'am" and "No, Ma'am" when responding to Eulalie and their relationship quickly improved to one of mutual respect, and even warmth. As Dooley began feeling better about himself and more comfortable with his teacher, he became a more eager learner. My mother told me that in reflecting on that year, she believed her greatest accomplishment as a teacher and as a human being came from the growth of her relationship to Dooley Sims.

As the chill of winter engulfed the little school in Orange, knifing in through the cracks in the walls, the stove at the rear center of Eulalie's classroom sprung to life. Keeping the fire going was the responsibility of the older youth who brought in wood from an outside shed and fed the stove as needed.

It was near the end of winter when my mother summoned up the courage to discard some of the drudgery of daily recitation, memorization and exercises, in order to share historical anecdotes with the children, most of which were not included in the textbooks she was required to use.

One of the stories she told her students was about a very beautiful quadroon slave woman named Sally Hemings, who was owned by Thomas Jefferson, the author of the Declaration of Independence and the third President of the United States.

She told them there would always be people who believed Mr. Jefferson was the father of Sally's seven children, a charge made public during Jefferson's presidency by a newspaper reporter named James T. Callender. The historical evidence rather strongly supported the reporter's account, although Jefferson himself neither confirmed nor denied it. Regardless of whether the relationship was ever proven or not, it was a story my mother always loved to tell, probably because it so closely paralleled her own genealogical history.

I remember her cheeks flushed red and her words spilled forth rapidly when she first told me about Thomas Jefferson and Sally Hemings --- how Mr. Jefferson reportedly first seduced the girl in Paris, where they lived while he was the United States Minister to France. Sally was then sixteen and Jefferson was in his early forties.

"You see, he brought Sally to Paris from Monticello, his plantation in Virginia, to be a maid to his daughter, Polly. It was there in Paris where Sally got pregnant with her first child, and when the child was born back in Virginia she named him Thomas Jefferson Hemings."

To support her belief that Jefferson was the father of Sally Hemings' children, Eulalie carefully noted that Sally conceived the rest of her children at Monticello and, every time she conceived Thomas Jefferson was right there at Monticello with her.

"In fact, when they returned from Paris, Sally became his personal maid and her sleeping quarters were adjacent to his."

Then there was the claimed physical resemblance to Thomas Jefferson of Sally's first son, who was born in 1790, and her last child, a boy named Easton, who was born in 1808. Both boys had the same red hair, blue eyes, facial features, and tall stature as Thomas Jefferson. Years after Sally died, Madison Hemings, her third son, who was named after James Madison, Thomas Jefferson's best friend, wrote in his memoirs that his mother confided in him that Jefferson was indeed his father, and the father of his siblings -- a fact all of Sally's progeny had learned through plantation gossip when they were children.

My mother said her students were so enthused over the Sally Hemings story that she had trouble controlling the discussion that followed. They wanted to know if all colored folks named Jefferson were blood relations of the former president. She told them no, certainly not all, "But who knows, a few could be."

Bertha, one of the teenaged students, said she knew of a black girl in Beaumont who got pregnant by a white man who owned a grocery store. "The yellow kid come outta her look jes like dat man."

Bertha's revelation sparked similar stories from others, until finally my mother had to stop the discussion when the older students started speculating on the parentage of fair-skinned colored children they knew in Orange. She told them it was not appropriate to gossip about local people. What she didn't tell them was that, as part of their study of history, she planned to share information on her own background, which she later did.

My mother believed teaching that year in Orange was a tremendous learning experience. Among many other things, she learned organizational skills, how to deal with children in a group setting, and how important it was to genuinely try to identify the individual needs of children and to respond to them as best you can. The experience also angered and saddened her because of the inadequacy of Negro education, and she was painfully aware that as an untrained eighteen-year-old teacher she was part of that inadequacy.

The money my mother earned as a teacher in Orange enabled her to enroll in Prairie View University, where she studied for the next two years, majoring in history and home economics.

# CHAPTER 9

# EULALIE AND JOHN

Mama Peachey instilled in her daughters the importance of marrying well-educated, cultured, gentlemen who showed substantial promise for achieving success. She told her girls they were less likely to find such men among darker-hued Negroes, given the realities of racial discrimination.

My grandmother's message to her daughters was powerfully underscored by the poverty and oppression which characterized most of the Negro world around them, and by the mixed-race backgrounds of most of the Negroes who were successful in partially transcending the race barrier.

Mama Peachey's instruction was also dramatically reinforced by the relative poverty of her own family; yet, the most tragic hammer blow of discrimination fell upon the proud and musically gifted Papa Peachey. Toiling away his final years as a low-paid menial worker, his dream of a musical career long dashed, Papa Peachey faced the sad likelihood that his sons would share his fate and see their hopes crushed beneath the racist heel.

All six of her daughters fulfilled Mama Peachey's most cherished hopes by marrying mulatto men with education and careers that promised solid financial security and, perhaps, even a taste of affluence.

The chosen husbands included a promising young Galveston dentist; the first colored railway mail clerk hired in Houston; my own father -- who had earned an advanced degree in pharmaceutic chemistry; an early Negro graduate of the University of California at Berkeley; the first Negro graduate of the University of California Hastings Law School -- who later became a very successful Los Angeles attorney; a civil engineer; and a socially and financially prominent Omaha, Nebraska veterinarian.

The third oldest of the sisters, my mother, was also the third to marry. She and my father, John Alvin Martin, were married on a Sunday afternoon in June 1930. The ceremony was performed in St. Nicholas Catholic Church in Houston, where my father had once been an altar boy.

The romance of Eulalie and John had a lovely boy-girl-next-door quality to it, with a discovery-rediscovery twist. They had known each other since childhood, lived in close proximity, and attended the same schools. John, who was two years older than Eulalie, had also been a sometime friend of her brother, Edward.

Mother said the first time my father walked her home from high school, one of her classmates, a girl named Verna Mae Jenkins, insisted on accompanying them. During the entire twenty minute walk, Verna Mae chattered on and on about the dumb things kids had done in school that day, while my mother and father ignored her and silently focused on each other.

As they neared the Peachey residence, Verna Mae's voice suddenly pierced the wall of silence erected by her companions. My mother remembered her saying, "Girl, what's wrong with you? You got your monthlies or somethin'? If you crampin,' you shoulda told me and not let me run on at the mouth like dat. I jus finish wit' mines, and Lord, I bled like a stuck pig, and it hurt me so I cried for two straight days. Is that what's ailin' you now, Eulalie? If it is, you might get some comfort from a hot water bottle on your belly. It didn't help me none, but my mama say it'll sometime help."

The fourteen-year-old Eulalie was mortified by Verna Mae's outburst on menstruation and cramps in the presence of a boy, any boy, but particularly one that she liked. She remembered her face feeling like it was on fire, and for a moment her breath got stuck in her throat. Then embarrassment and humiliation quickly turned to anger.

She told Verna Mae she felt fine. And with a voice steeped in scorn, my mother added that she simply wasn't interested in listening to someone babble on about the stupid antics of a bunch of dumb kids.

My mother laughed as she recalled Verna Mae looking at her in wide-eyed, open-mouthed disbelief. She was obviously more stunned and surprised than hurt, since most of what she and Eulalie talked about enthusiastically every day after school were the stupid antics of dumb kids. But my father didn't know that at the time, and my mother wanted to impress him with her maturity, as well as vent her wrath on Verna Mae.

Her face still red, my mother said she thanked my father for walking with her and apologized to him, in front of Verna Mae, for the stupid background noise they endured while walking. Then, without a look or a word for Verna Mae, my mother turned and ran the last few yards to her house.

For the remainder of the academic year, John and Eulalie always greeted each other warmly when their paths crossed at school and, occasionally, they stopped to talk in the hallways between classes. Several times they ate lunch together. My mother said that she and my father liked each other from the start. She said their teenage relationship was characterized by a sweet innocence, which she treasured long afterwards.

My parents had similar recollections of a day in June near the end of the 1923 school year. They walked to my mother's house alone that day, mostly talking about my father going away to Howard University in September and his desire to become a scientist or a physician. He wasn't sure which career he'd choose, but he was very excited about the academic challenges awaiting him.

He suspected he would be homesick for a short while, but the idea of living and studying in Washington, D.C. was something he could hardly wait to experience. The very idea of being in the same city as the White House, the Lincoln Memorial, the Smithsonian Institute, and the U.S. Congress, was mind boggling to my father, who was sixteen at the time.

My mother told me her thoughts that day were bittersweet. She was genuinely happy that John would have the opportunity to attend Howard. He was such a brilliant boy, class valedictorian and all, that it would have been a crime if he had not gone on to higher learning. And Howard was the very best of the Negro colleges. It was so very fortunate that John's father had the money and the commitment to send his son to Howard, she recalled thinking as they leisurely walked Fourth Ward streets to her house.

My mother said she was also sad that the boy she liked so much was leaving Houston. Her instincts told her their relationship was likely to change, if not end, with his departure. He would be exposed to new, interesting, smart people. He would make new friends, meet new girls, and maybe even fall in love. It was possible he might never return to Houston to live permanently. She might even be spending her very last minutes with John.

For his part, my father told me he found tremendous satisfaction in talking to my mother that day. She was not only a good listener, but he sensed she understood and appreciated his excitement about going off to Howard. Some of his less accomplished and poorer peers resented and envied him because of his academic success, along with the fact that his father could afford to send him away to a prestigious college. This sort of backlash made him very circumspect when talking to others about himself. But Eulalie seemed so genuinely happy for him that she made it easy for him to share his enthusiasm and excitement with her.

I asked my father whether he sensed my mother was also sad over his leaving. He replied that they both acknowledged they would miss each other, and he recalled telling her he would always consider her a special friend.

Late in August 1923, my father left for Washington, D.C. to begin his undergraduate studies at Howard University. A week later, my mother began her sophomore year at Booker T. Washington High. Each wrote to the other once during the beginning of the 1923-1924 school year, and my father visited the Peachey residence one afternoon during his first Christmas vacation home. That was the extent of their contact that year and for the next six years.

In 1926 Eulalie graduated from high school. At that time she was going steady with Robert Tidwell, a Houston native and a fellow graduate of Booker T. Washington High. Robert was in his second year at Fisk University in Tennessee. He came home from college in time to escort my mother to her senior prom, and during the summer of 1926 he was a frequent visitor at the Peachey's house on Nelson Street.

Mama Peachey liked Robert Tidwell, who came from a prominent family. His father, Richard Tidwell, was part owner of the Western Star Publishing Company, which published a monthly newsletter for Negroes. Robert was a well-mannered young mulatto who aspired to be a physician, and Mama Peachey took to him right away. Here was exactly the sort of man she had long advised her daughters to marry, and the prospect that her darling Eulalie might land such a catch had her dancing around the house.

My mother liked Robert, but she didn't think she loved him. In any event, she wasn't ready for marriage to Robert or anyone else. When he proposed in the summer of 1926, she told him of her plans to teach school in Orange, Texas before attending college. Robert suggested they could have a long engagement, but my mother declined, saying that she just wasn't ready to make that commitment.

Meanwhile, halfway across the country in Washington, D.C., John Martin and a Howard classmate named Lena Williams had fallen in love during their freshman year. Remembering this long ago love, my father once wrote: "Lena was my college sweetheart, my first real sweetheart. She was a fine person, in my opinion a magnificent person, and for three years I loved her with all the ardor of my being."

Just as my mother did not marry Robert Tidwell, my father did not marry Lena Williams, although the end of their relationships came in different ways. While Eulalie's decision not to marry Robert Tidwell was entirely hers, John was pressured by his parents into ending his relationship with Lena Williams. My grandparents told my father that he had a moral responsibility to them to pursue and finish his education, unimpeded by a wife or fiancée. The former Catholic altar boy's strong sense of familial obligation left him no choice but to comply with his parents wishes.

In June 1929, my mother returned to Houston after completing two years of study at Prairie View University. She hoped to work that summer, and perhaps longer, to earn enough money to return to college and complete her degree. That same June, my father, after earning his undergraduate degree three years earlier, graduated from the Howard University College of Pharmacy and was eagerly considering two attractive job offers from pharmaceutical laboratories in Baltimore and Philadelphia.

Once again, his parents intervened. "Come home, son," I imagine them saying. "We've provided for your education, now we need you. We're getting old, and you must care for us when we can no longer care for ourselves."

My Grandpa Martin was then sixty, Grandma Martin was fifty-four, and they both had another thirty years of healthy life in front of them. Of course, my father had no way of knowing that. So the promising young scientist responded in character to the plaintive plea of his parents. He returned home to Houston and took a job his father had procured for him as a Negro drugstore pharmacist.

Independently, Eulalie and John gravitated to a group of Houston young people each had known since childhood. Most were from mulatto backgrounds, all were in their early to mid-twenties, and all had attended Negro colleges. Often from affluent families, they were considered the

elite of Houston's young adult Negro community. So it came to pass that Eulalie and John rediscovered each other while in the process of renewing old childhood friendships. Only, in their case, friendship quickly blossomed into love.

About two hundred people attended the wedding of Eulalie Helen Peachey and John Alvin Martin at St. Nicholas Catholic Church. The two sets of

*Eulalie and John*

parents sat across the aisle from each other with smiles of pride and approval on their faces. The invited guests consisted of family, friends and acquaintances of the bride and groom, and their respective parents, along with a cadre of St. Nicholas parishioners who attended every event at the church, whether invited or not.

The newlyweds enjoyed a three-day honeymoon in Galveston before moving into the home of the groom's parents at 118 West Gray Avenue in Houston. It was planned as a temporary stay until my father could obtain a full-time position. Unfortunately, sometime before the wedding, the impact of the Great Depression had stifled business in the drugstore where my father worked, forcing his employer to reduce Dad's hours. My parent's dream of buying a home had to be put on hold.

My mother remembered Grandma Martin as being meddlesome from the outset, offering daily opinions on everything from personal grooming and cooking to church attendance and their social life. Fortunately, my mother continued to work for awhile as an inventory clerk in a downtown department store, and that greatly reduced the time she spent at home. Nevertheless, she began early on to experience lingering periods of depression, which she attributed primarily to the living arrangement with her in-laws, although the phased migration of the Peachey family to Berkeley, California was also a factor.

Three years before Eulalie and John married, Tom, Jr. left Houston for California, settling in the Oakland-Berkeley Bay Area. A year later, Brother followed. In June 1930, Brother returned to Houston in a Ford sedan to attend my mother's wedding and sister Irene's high school graduation. That same summer, Mama Peachey and her two youngest daughters, Irene and Winona, packed their personal belongings into Brother's Ford and drove back with him to California. Papa Peachey and twenty-year-old Maudell followed by train. The destination for the Peachey émigrés was Berkeley, where Tom, Jr. had rented a three-bedroom house for the family at 2814 Dohr Street.

Louise and Bessie, Eulalie's two older sisters, remained in Houston with their families. Although having Louise and Bessie around was comforting for my mother, her life was inevitably different from the old days on Nelson Street. She missed her parents and siblings terribly. This longing for her family and the dissatisfaction of living with her in-laws often resulted in Eulalie experiencing long periods of depression.

The silver that lined the gray was her love for her husband. There was absolutely no doubt in her mind that she loved him, and that he loved her. She said she felt it when she looked at him, when she listened to him talk and laugh, and when she saw the reflection of herself in his eyes.

My mother told me my father was the most sensitive, thoughtful man she ever knew. "Lines from Shakespeare or a poem which touched John often brought tears to his eyes," she said. "After we married, he tried extra hard to be aware of my feelings and, whenever he thought I was depressed, he would insist we go out to visit friends, see a movie, take an automobile ride, anything he thought would cheer me up. From the beginning, my spirits were inevitably lifted whenever he got me out of his parents house."

Without the slightest hint of embarrassment, my mother spoke to me of intimate details of her life with my father. Only many years later, as I approached middle age, did I realize how wonderfully unusual it was for a mother to speak so openly about such matters to a son.

She told me that there were the painful and awkward beginning exercises in sex, which her virginity and his relative inexperience magnified. But that their lovemaking quickly left that starting place and carried them beyond fantasy to an ecstasy of the senses neither had ever come close to experiencing, or even contemplating. She began to feel his presence and his touch even when he was not there.

She cherished the evenings they drove to the waterfront and watched sunsets in silence, or sat on a park bench eating ice cream, talking earnestly about their future. They also enjoyed being surrounded by trees and grass and the laughter of other young lovers strolling on the path in front of them. On one such evening, while seated on their favorite park bench, they witnessed a scene they both remembered for many years.

A black man in his forties approached, walking slowly several yards in front of a woman. He was handsome, erect and his prominently chiseled Indian-like features accented a look of utter contentment as he drew deeply on a cigarette and studied the sky above him. The woman's dark-brown weathered countenance displayed an angry scowl as she limped along with a pained, bowlegged gait several yards behind the man.

As she neared the bench where Eulalie and John sat holding hands, she shouted at the man in front of her, totally oblivious to her public surroundings. My mother remembered her saying, "You so rough when we do it. You hurt me an' ack like you 'joy hurtin' me. Ain't you got no sof feelin' for me at'al?"

According to Mother, the man said nothing in response to the woman's outburst, nor did he turn to look at her, or wait for her to come abreast of him, or quicken his pace to distance himself from her. He continued to exhale smoke and study the sky with an aura that suggested his connection to that particular woman would always be on his terms, and his alone.

Initially, Eulalie and John stifled embarrassed laughs. Later, after they'd had a chance for thoughtful reflection, they talked over the incident and came to a fuller appreciation of the mutual caring and respect that characterized their deep love. They were thankful that they had each other, and they vowed to approach every day of their lives with a renewed commitment to each other, and to never take the other's love for granted.

# Chapter 10

# Breakdown

I was born at 4:40 p.m. on November 24, 1931, in Houston Colored Hospital. I turned out to be Eulalie and John's only child. When I was a small boy my mother occasionally informed me that my birth had been a particularly arduous and painful experience for her. As a result, I had a responsibility to be a good boy and not cause her additional grief.

Before I was born, my mother had been the center of attention in the Martin household, although she did not always welcome it. While she reveled in the nurturing of her sensitive, loving husband, her reaction to the attentions of her in-laws was more complex.

Her relationship to her father-in-law sometimes reminded her of the childhood friendship she enjoyed with Mr. Tomkins, the ill-fated candy storeowner. Whenever Mr. Martin looked at her, he did so with a broad smile of genuine fatherly approval. Like Mr. Tomkins, Grandpa Martin enjoyed listening to and talking with his daughter-in-law. They sometimes sat on the front porch together sipping lemonade and discussing family matters, the events of the day, or whatever was of interest to them. Eulalie came to believe that Mr. Martin loved her as though she were his very own daughter and that he would do whatever he could to help make her happy.

Unlike his wife, Grandpa Martin was sympathetic with the young couple's desire to live apart from parents. But he realized that the economic chaos in the country made their current extended family living arrangement necessary.

He reasoned, incorrectly, however, that the Depression alone was responsible for his well-educated son being unable to support a separate household, and that Houston's horrendous racial discrimination had little or nothing to do with it. So my grandfather, whose modest assets had been left unscathed by the Depression, hoped to help his son and daughter-in-law by giving them a vacant lot he was about to purchase in the Fifth Ward. And later, when his son's earnings increased to an appropriate level, he planned to help John build a house on the lot.

In contrast to her father-in-law, my mother found her omnipresent mother-in-law overbearing, meddlesome and even a little jealous of her son's relationship to his wife. It wasn't that my mother believed Grandma Martin disliked her, because clearly the opposite was true. The problem was my grandmother's inability to let go of her son, and her tendency to treat my mother like a child rather than her son's wife. This made living in my grandmother's house increasingly intolerable for my mother.

As far as Grandma Martin was concerned, the children, as she called them, could have lived under her roof forever. As long as they weren't cramped for space, she saw no reason for them to ever move away from 118 West Gray Avenue. And if living space became too tight after the children had kids of their own, Grandma Martin hoped to convince her husband to build an additional room onto their house. She saw no need for John and Eulalie to live apart from her.

My mother said the attention showered on her during her pregnancy by all three Martins was often overwhelming. Her own mother's pregnancies were so frequent that a certain business-as-usual attitude surrounded them. Nevertheless, each of Mama Peachey's deliveries were considered blessed events by her family. "But we didn't go nuts like the Martin's did when I was carrying you," she told me.

"It was as if I was carrying royalty in my belly. Mrs. Martin followed me around that house like a puppy. The bathroom was my only sanctuary, and then it would be only for a few minutes before I'd hear her voice telling me how long I had been in there and asking me if I was alright. When you started kicking inside me, it seemed like I constantly had a hand on my abdomen, mostly your father's, which I welcomed, or your grandmother's, which often annoyed me. Mr. Martin was respectful and shy. He waited for me to invite him to feel his grandson kick. He always respected my privacy and treated me like an adult, whereas Grandma Martin was the opposite. In spite of my protests, she treated me like a child who was in constant need of her attention."

Mother said my birth unleashed an array of new emotions in her. In addition to a sense of emptiness, which she later attributed to the end of her pregnancy, her feelings were hurt by what she perceived as a major shift in attention from her to the newborn infant. "As annoying as the prebirth attention was, I still felt hurt when it stopped after your birth."

Mother said she also continued to see the Peachey's move to California as an act of abandonment. "How could my own family have deserted me?" she remembered repeatedly moaning, while weeping bitter tears of hurt and sorrow. Those periods of self-pity were apparently symptomatic of Eulalie's postpartum depression. In her case, the depression went well beyond the fleeting, often inexplicable, sadness which many women experience following the birth of their first child.

Yet my mother's descent into depression was not an instant plunge following my birth. "After the ordeal of birthing you, I felt a tremendous sense of relief," she said. "I was physically exhausted and happy at the same time. When you first took the nipple of my breast into your tiny mouth, it felt joyously natural to me. Then a day or so later I started to feel hollow, empty inside, like I had lost something, and I'd cry for no reason at all."

I'll never forget being mesmerized by my mother's account of the depression she suffered after my birth. While I cannot recall her exact words I'll always remember the substance and vivid details of that story.

"I'd just start crying uncontrollably. After we got home from the hospital, I didn't really feel like I was at home, but rather in some foreign place. John's parents and relatives seemed like total strangers, dark-skinned strangers, who kept taking my baby from my arms and mouthing an incomprehensible Louisiana sounding gibberish. Some of those people were as black as the ace of spades, not my people at all. I didn't want them touching you and, at the same time, I felt ashamed of my feelings toward them.

"The second week after I returned home from the hospital, I had this horrible dream in which I fell into a pit of black snakes. The serpents covered every inch of my body, including my face and head. I couldn't move or see anything but blackness. I woke up screaming, and John held and comforted me the rest of the night. God, that was a terrible dream."

It was during this time that my mother's longing for Mama Peachey was most intense, and she cried a great deal because she could not satisfy that longing. She said her mood improved when Louise or Bessie visited, or when she left the Martin's house to visit them, or to see friends.

"During those visits with my sisters, or the friends I had known since childhood, I actually felt like my old self," she remembered. "But as soon as I returned home, I would almost immediately revert to a state of sadness. It was just intolerable to have those sudden, unexpected shifts in mood."

Family and friends attributed my mother's early symptoms of depression to a slow recovery from childbirth. It was not unusual, they reasoned, for some young women to have lingering emotional side effects following the birth of a first child. The best approach was to treat her as if nothing was wrong and she would soon be her old self again. In the meantime, there was a healthy, active baby to care for.

"You were a lovely baby, Johnny. I wanted so much in my heart to be your sole caregiver but, after a short while, I couldn't do it alone and your father's help wasn't quite enough. I needed Grandma Martin, and boy she was right there taking you out of my arms or your crib whenever she wanted, and I felt relieved and resentful at the same time. My feelings of loneliness, isolation and uselessness intensified, particularly when John was at work."

When I was about a year old, my mother's sporadic depression became constant and more pronounced.

"It wasn't a steady progression from tolerable to intolerable. I just remember I woke up one morning and it was a major struggle to get out of bed to go to the bathroom. When I left the bathroom, I immediately returned to bed, totally exhausted. The exhaustion didn't come and go. It stayed with me. I was too tired to eat. I couldn't even sit up in bed and read. I had trouble carrying on a conversation with John without feeling utterly drained. I just lay in bed and cried. This went on for weeks, and all the while my brain was telling me how worthless I was. I was worthless as a mother, as a wife, as a daughter-in-law, as a sister, and as a friend.

"I had this sense that everyone around me believed all I needed to do was to use willpower to force myself back into normalcy. I remember Louise saying, 'Honey, maybe you should be a little more determined about getting out of bed, going outside for some fresh air, and then cooking John a meal. I'm sure if you tried to return to your regular routine, you'd feel better.' If Louise had only known how hard I tried. I rose one day and walked unsteadily into the kitchen determined to make something for my husband's dinner, only to fall exhausted into a kitchen chair and feel more useless than ever."

Joseph Gathings, the attending physician during my birth, decided Mother was having a nervous breakdown. She was taken to a hospital in Prairie View, Texas a short distance from Houston, where she stayed for about a month. Not surprisingly, her recovery away from the Martin family home was as complete as it was rapid.

Following her release from the hospital, my mother became more determined to get my father to explore other employment options. The Third Ward drugstore, where he hung his pharmacy degree and occasionally filled prescriptions, seemed constantly on the verge of going out of business. In the two and one half years they had been married, his base salary had not significantly increased. Making more money was the key to their liberation from the Martin family residence and Mother had come to believe their early departure was crucial for their happiness, and for her mental health.

My father agreed that my mother's restored health was the top priority for both of them. He told me that he cried tears of sheer joy when he realized she was well again. The animation in her eyes, the strength in her arms as she embraced him, and the quickness in her step as they left the hospital were the first wondrous signs that his beautiful young wife, whom he loved without reservation, had successfully broken the steely grip of depression.

After coming home from the hospital, Eulalie talked incessantly about their need to live apart from his parents and for John to seek other employment. He said he was so enraptured by having her back to normal, that he tended to nod agreement to everything she said. He reveled in her wellness. While her goals for their little family were generally his goals as well, my father disagreed with my mother about the timing. While she wanted immediate change, he didn't believe that was practical or even possible.

He was well aware that despite being one of the most highly educated Negroes in Houston, he was still stuck in an unrewarding job. He frequently thought about the research positions in Baltimore and Philadelphia he had turned down to return to Houston at his parents urging.

Surely his scientific knowledge was worth more than dispensing pills. He didn't like the status quo any more than Eulalie did. But beyond the fact that this was racist Houston, the entire country was in the throes of an economic depression. People everywhere were out of work and times were universally hard.

His lovely, impatient wife seemed to ignore that reality. She acted as if this wasn't the Houston she had lived in all of her life, that they weren't colored, and that there was no economic depression. She believed John should be able to stick his degrees under any employer's nose and walk away with a prestigious position. He was confident things would eventually work out well for them, but they needed to be patient. "In the meantime," he frequently told Eulalie, "we must make the best of our current circumstances."

"Son, you can't believe how wonderful it felt to be well," my mother often said when reflecting on that period of her life. "It was the greatest feeling to be able to care for you, to love my husband, and to laugh with my sisters and friends.

"At the same time, I knew my health problems were connected to living with the Martins, and Louise and Bessie agreed.

'Girl, you need to pack up JohnnyBoy and that less than enterprising husband of yours, and get your three butts out of that house before you go permanently crazy,' one or both of my sisters would say."

My mother said, "I just couldn't move us on my own, and I knew John and I didn't have the money to sustain an independent lifestyle. The days and weeks turned into months. I could feel the old depression and lethargy coming on, but I was determined not to give in to it this time. It was Louise who first suggested that I take a trip to California. I had thought about it before she mentioned it, but I was torn. I didn't want to go on vacation without your father, but my sisters convinced me it was the right thing to do for my health."

When my mother floated the idea of taking a trip to California to visit the Peacheys, my father unhesitatingly endorsed it, as did his parents. All three Martins thought such a visit would be a tremendous boon to my mother's ongoing recovery. It would give her an opportunity to see the grandeur of California for the first time in her life, while spending a month with the Peacheys and giving them their first opportunity to see her baby boy.

As a Southern Pacific employee, Grandpa Martin was entitled to railroad travel passes for himself and family members, so a round trip ticket from Houston to Berkeley, California wouldn't cost a cent. My parents wanted to go to California together but, since my father's job didn't provide vacation pay, it was decided that he would remain in Houston to continue working.

In August 1933, my mother and I boarded a Southern Pacific passenger train in Houston and were ushered into a segregated day-coach for Negroes. If my mother had traveled without me, she probably could have avoided the indignity of that segregated coach -- although doing so wouldn't have occurred to her. After all, she had lived every day of her twenty-five years as a Negro in the racially segregated south. I was twenty-one months old when we left my father and grandparents standing on the station platform, waving goodbye. Everyone thought the separation would only last a month. But one month turned into many and my father and I would not see each other again for six long years.

## CHAPTER 11

# FANTASY AND MEMORY

As I reflect on my very earliest memories of Mother and myself, my mind produces only happy pictures of long ago events. I have no problem with the likelihood that my mental images are based on stories Mother told me, embellished by my fantasies, rather than my memory of the actual events. They were the kind of sweet snippets of toddler days which I never tired of hearing my mother describe. In fact, as a small boy, I so delighted in Mother's reminisces of those post-infancy days that I often asked her to repeat the stories. One of my favorite anecdotes involved a set of toy blocks.

*Eulalie & son, John, Jr. in Berkeley, California, circa 1933*

"Tell me again, Mother, about my ABC blocks on the train."

Mother would smile, soak in my eagerness with warm brown eyes, then repeat the story of how I, at twenty-one-months of age, threw my alphabet play blocks out of the windows of that Southern Pacific passenger train during our trip from Houston to Berkeley in August 1933 Mother said I hurled the blocks one at a time over several hundred miles and after each throw I'd press my nose against the glass window to see my former possession hit the ground beside the train track, roll down the embankment and out of sight.   I would then turn to Mother with a look which said, boy that was fun, but I want my block back now.

"You really loved those blocks, but you just couldn't resist seeing them fly through the air from that moving train. I couldn't stop you from throwing them because I never knew the exact moment you'd be possessed by the irresistible urge to toss one out the window."

My memory of the alphabet block-throwing story was dreamily revised over the years. Early on, say around five years old, I saw myself as I appeared in a photo taken when I was eighteen months of age: a large smile on my face, hair slicked down and parted in the middle, clad in white shorts and white jersey top, seated on the train next to the window with an alphabet block in hand ready to be pitched. Then I'm throwing the block up and out of the top lowered window and watching it twist and turn in the air as it falls to a graveled embankment.

When I was six and a half years old and once again actually riding the train on that same Southern Pacific line between California and Texas, I added texture and depth to the old block-throwing story. In this later fantasy there was a white-jacketed porter ambling down the aisle with a broad friendly smile on his face, informing the passengers of how many minutes to the next stop. The porter stops beside our seat and engages my mother in conversation.  As their idle chitchat continues, Mother's attention is no longer focused on me.  So I throw another alphabet block through the slightly opened upper window. The porter laughs, Mother is exasperated by my behavior and I'm thrilled by the flight of my toy, then saddened by its loss.

At fifteen, during that same train journey, my fantasized memory of the ABC's block-throwing episode focused on Mother. There she was those many years ago sitting next to my toddler self in all her loveliness, patiently saying, "Sweetheart, you mustn't throw any more of your blocks out the window. Mother can't stop the train to go find them, Baby, so when you throw them away, we'll never see them again."

Mother has her left arm around me, pulling me close to cuddle. I look up into her pretty, fair-complexioned face and she smiles and kisses my forehead. She isn't angry with me for tossing my toy blocks, she's only concerned about the enjoyment I'll miss due to their loss. And suddenly I visualize the presence of that young version of my mother. She is seated next to me and we are happily riding the Southern Pacific back to the husband and father we left long ago. The fantasy quickly ends as the train enters a dark tunnel along the route of the discarded alphabet blocks of fourteen years past.

There were, of course, other anecdotes of my pre-three-year-old life my mother enjoyed sharing with me. I've probably forgotten many of them, but others were so firmly implanted in my memory that, sixty years after the fact, I continue to believe I'm recalling the actual events as they happened.

I remember Mother telling me that George Dean, my very best boyhood friend, and his mother, Ivy, also came to California from Texas around the same time we did. As my friendship with George grew, I invented a joyous fiction in which he and I traveled to California together, having great fun throughout the journey.

Then there were the early weeks and months in Berkeley which, for me, according to Mother who had taken a job in an Oakland clothing store, were centered around my grandmother, Mama Peachey, and two of my aunts, Maudell and Winona. I adored my mother's family and each member showered me with kindness and love. Of course, my earliest recollections of life in the Peachey household are fragmented.

I remember my play automobile. It was red and I routinely pedaled it under Mama Peachey's kitchen sink, which I called my gadage (garage). There was my mother's brother, Tom, who took me for rides in his car and treated me to ice cream cones. I remember Tom and I making a solemn pledge to each other that we would always be "pals." Tom even suggested that we address each other as Pal, which we did off and on for several years.

Early on I was exposed to the stories of Mama Peachey being mistaken for white by people she encountered while shopping or riding city buses. Since my mother (who had similar experiences) and other family members derived such ironic enjoyment from hearing these stories, I automatically liked them, too.

The most prized stories typically involved some white woman Mama Peachey didn't know who happened to be seated beside my grandmother on a city bus. The stranger and Mama would generally be engaged in innocuous small talk when suddenly the white lady would

*Maud White (Mama) Peachey*

launch into a racist diatribe against Negroes and their growing presence in the Bay Area.

Undoubtedly, the specific words of Mama Peachey's seat companions differed, but the general thrust of their remarks was probably similar to the following: "Why, they're just overrunning this area and bringing all of their loud-mouthed ignorance, filth and crime with them. And no one is doing anything about it. If it were left to me, I'd send all the black bastards back to Africa. God, don't you just hate them?"

109

Mama Peachey would usually allow her bigoted seat partner to ramble on in this fashion for a good while without saying a word herself. Then, at some point, usually when her seat companion paused to savor her own venom, Mama would get her voluble companion's attention, fix the woman with a steely-eyed stare, and say something like, "Madam, I am a Negro. And most of the white-looking people on this bus probably have Negro blood, just like me. You didn't know that, did you Honey? Maybe the best thing for you to do is get your white-trash butt off this bus right now. And the next best thing you can do is to get rid of all that hate you got stored in your heart."

"Did Miss White Trash get off the bus, Mama?" one of her adult brood would laughingly ask. Most of the time the answer was no, but when Mama said yes, hands would clap and everyone would roar with happy laughter.

Thus, the primary enemy was defined for me at a very early age. They were ignorant white people who talked hatefully about colored people. But I wondered how I would recognize those evil folks unless I heard them saying bad things to Mama or my mother on a city bus. Somehow I knew instinctively that all white people weren't to be categorized as bad. Once I asked my mother how I could distinguish the good white people from the bad ones. She hugged me and said, "You'll know, because the bad ones have many, many ways of letting you know how truly hateful they are."

CHAPTER 12

# CALIFORNIA FREEDOM

Life for the Peacheys proved far more sanguine in the San Francisco Bay Area than it was, or was ever likely to be, in Houston. The working class residential neighborhood in southwest Berkeley, where the family settled after leaving Houston, had paved, tree-lined streets and sturdy well-kept frame houses. In the 1930s, whites, Asians, mulattoes and blacks lived side-by-side in southwest Berkeley, generally without interracial rancor or tension.

There was an anti-miscegenation law in California until the State Supreme Court declared it unconstitutional in 1948. There were also racially restrictive covenants on residential property located in specific areas of Berkeley. But the pervasive patterns of legal segregation, which characterized the South, were nonexistent in Berkeley. This, of course, made it less imperative in lower income, working class neighborhoods to carefully discern who was white and who was black.

The modest two-story Peachey residence at 2814 Dohr Street had three upstairs bedrooms, inside plumbing and one and a half baths. In all, it boasted three more rooms than the house on Nelson Street in Houston, where Mama and Papa Peachey raised their eight children. The property included an unattached garage and a productive apricot tree in the backyard, which Papa Peachey considered a special friend in the solitude of his old age. In 1930, my grandparents rented the Dohr Street house for seven dollars and fifty cents per week.

Two of my aunts, Maudell, then twenty-two, and seventeen-year-old Winona (Nonie) lived with Mama and Papa in the house on Dohr Street, when Mother and I arrived in August, 1933. Irene, who was twenty, had recently moved into an apartment on Alcatraz Avenue in Berkeley, following her March marriage to James F. Davis. Edward (Brother) had developed an immediate love affair with San Francisco. There, he lived and worked and led the life of a party-going young single, while attempting to establish himself as a musician. Tom, Jr. lived in Oakland, where he worked as an assistant mechanic in an auto repair shop. Papa Peachey, who was sixty-five at the time Mother and I arrived in Berkeley, was employed as a porter at the Athens Club in Oakland, while Mama Peachey had resumed her role as the ever-essential homemaker.

Maudell and Nonie both proudly claimed a share of the credit for starting the Peachey practice of giving me my morning milk by attaching nursing nipples to whiskey, gin or wine bottles. They justified this

*Aunt Maudell*

decidedly unorthodox practice as an appropriate Depression-era response to my habit of tossing my regular glass nursing bottles out of a second floor bedroom window. As a result of Papa Peachey's drinking, and the frequent partying of his sons and daughters, empty liquor bottles were in abundant supply in the Peachey household, in contrast to a dearth of nursing bottles.

My grandmother was happy with her new life in Berkeley. She

consistently hummed tunes to herself as she bustled about the house, cleaning, preparing meals, and caring for me during the day. Mama's neighbors and local merchants alike, especially the corner grocer on Russell Street, an Italian named Al, and King, the Chinese owner of the larger Sacramento Street market, regarded Mama warmly. Both saved special cuts of meat and their freshest produce for my grandmother.

By this time, Daughter had also moved to Oakland and the two cousins saw each other frequently, often at 11 o'clock Sunday services at the African-Methodist Episcopal Church on 15th street in Oakland, which they both attended regularly.

In the beginning of their new life in Berkeley, Papa Peachey enjoyed a brief, albeit spirited, participation in The Townsend Movement, a nationwide grassroots political organization founded by Dr. Francis E. Townsend as an economic response to the Great Depression. Papa Peachey, like the other 800,000 Townsend adherents, was attracted to the organization's goal of providing every American citizen over age sixty with $200 each month. The money was to be spent within the month it was received, thereby helping to stimulate the drastically depressed American economy.

But following his short-lived involvement as a door-to-door membership solicitor for the Townsend Movement, Papa Peachey's life became considerably less active. He began to spend almost all of his time alone in the smallest, and most isolated, of the upstairs bedrooms. He would sit in a chair next to his bed reading newspapers, sipping cheap wine and listening to the radio. Generally, no one disturbed him, except to call him to meals. Occasionally, in the evening, he could be found at the piano in the dining room playing "Danny Boy" or some other sad ode to the unfulfilled dreams of his youth.

I don't know when my mother first decided on her either-or plan to force my father to leave Houston and move to Berkeley. I know my father believed our Berkeley trip was strictly intended as a short-term visit with relatives, and not a marital separation.

But once in Berkeley, again living with her parents and strongly encouraged by all five of her sisters, my mother decided to attempt to convince my father to move to Berkeley. Her resolve was further buttressed after she met a young couple named Elsie and Byron Rumford, who lived a few houses away from the Peachey residence.

Byron, like my father, was a university educated and licensed pharmacist, a somewhat rare educational and professional attainment

*John Alvin Martin*

for Negroes in the 1930s. Rumford had plans for opening a retail drug business on Sacramento Street, in the heart of southwest Berkeley. According to my mother, he was eager to meet my father and intrigued by the idea of a possible business partnership with him. My mother was ecstatic over the prospect and she thought my father would be equally enthusiastic.

Bursting with news of this potential business opportunity and prepared to regale my father with the beauty and wonders of the San Francisco Bay Area, my mother returned to Houston early in September 1933. She was confident of convincing her husband to leave Houston and resettle in Berkeley. She had also decided that if he refused to move west, she would leave him and, in effect, that is what she told him. She underscored her ultimatum by leaving me in Berkeley with Mama Peachey.

I once asked my father if, by this time, he had become disillusioned with his marriage and no longer loved Mother; if her ultimatum gave him a convenient way out.

"No, Johnny," he quickly replied. "I loved Eulalie with all my heart. I just couldn't submit to blackmail. She was totally inflexible. I was stunned, hurt, devastated and angry. And my masculine pride was definitely bruised.

"In spite of my feelings, I was still tempted to do what Eulalie wanted. But I knew if I had come to California as a result of her threat, your mother wouldn't have respected me in the long run, and I certainly wouldn't have respected myself."

In the beginning, I don't think my mother ever seriously believed my father would allow his wife and son to slip away. She knew he was tightly bound to his parents, particularly his mother, but she assumed his love for his wife and son was significantly stronger than his reluctance to leave Houston. It was a seriously flawed assumption.

"You know, Johnny, I loved your father, and I'm sure he loved me, but I don't think he understood as clearly as I that my sanity depended upon our not living with his parents. If I had been older and wiser, I probably wouldn't have sprung it on him in the way I did, but you have to understand that I felt a sense of desperation. In the final analysis, if your father had loved and wanted us enough, he would have joined us out here."

It was true. My father could have saved the marriage and kept our family together, if that was what he had really

*Eulalie at the beach*

wanted. At the time it all happened, I was, of course, too young to hate him. And, later, I acquired a stepfather I truly loved. As time passed, and my relationship with my stepfather changed, it made more sense to me to blame my mother for everything that was wrong in my life, past and present, and never my father, whom I really didn't know.

And when my father did reinsert himself in my life, many years later, I was in need of being rescued. Timing helped to make him my hero, and his earlier cowardly act of turning his back on Mother and me simply had no visceral meaning for me.

At the time of her ultimatum to her husband, my mother, with the help of her sister, Maudell, was quickly developing an active Bay Area social life, which included a number of unmarried and amorous young colored men from Maudell's stable of admirers. To what extent the presence of these potential backups gave Mother the courage to force the issue with her husband, I can only speculate.

The cold fact is that Eulalie's mulatto beauty was considered the ultimate female prize a colored man could win. She was mostly white, but America had defined her as black, which made her fair game for colored men. Character was probably of minimal consideration to many of the young colored men who pursued her, because her whiteness and physical beauty would have blinded them to all else.

Eulalie, through her mother's teaching and her own experiences, was acutely aware of her exalted status among colored men. Surrounded by these eager young men, she issued the ultimatum to her husband and, in the short-run, probably did not despair over its failure.

In October, my mother filed for dissolution of her marriage to my father. She also took a job as a retail salesperson at Lane Bryant, a women's apparel store in downtown Oakland, meanwhile continuing to enjoy the attentions of the google-eyed young colored men.

The four women of the house, Mama Peachey, Maudell, Nonie, and my mother, took turns caring for me, although my two aunts laughingly claimed my mother's major activities during this period were more man than child-oriented. An active social life, they all undoubtedly reasoned, tended to blunt the pain of divorce.

My mother continued to work daily at Lane Bryant during most of 1934. It was there, according to a story Nonie told me shortly after Mother's death, that she first met a young Italian-American named Angelo Monti, who was looking for a dress for his sister's birthday.

According to Nonie, it was a case of instant mutual attraction, although Eulalie later admitted that at the time she was both confused and anxious because Angelo was white. Racial segregation in Houston was so rigid that not one of the Peachey girls had ever had even a passing friendship with a white male.

Now, for the first time in her life, my mother was outside of the South and she found herself interacting at work with all kinds of people, including white males. Still, she was taken aback when this polite, respectful, good-looking young white man told

*The Peachey Family in Berkeley. Left to right from bottom, Mama, Papa, Eulalie, Bessie, Louise, Tom, Jr., Nonie, Maudell, Irene, Edward (Brother)*

her with a shy smile that, although the sister he was shopping for was about the same size as Eulalie, she wasn't as pretty.

Following that first encounter, Nonie said the two kept running into each other on the street or in the 10th Street Market, where Angelo was temporarily working, and where my mother often did the family grocery shopping. Each time they met they stopped to talk. Within a couple of weeks they were having lunch together, and sharing information on their respective backgrounds.

They began dating before Christmas, usually going to the movies or having dinner in Oakland or Berkeley during the week, and then crossing the Bay to enjoy the beauty of San Francisco on weekends. Angelo lived alone in the city in a small North Beach studio apartment near the home of his parents. His mom and dad turned out to be genuinely warm, accepting people who quickly helped Eulalie overcome her anxiety at meeting Angelo's family.

Angelo exposed Eulalie to delightfully new experiences: the San Francisco Opera, Golden Gate Park, dancing at the Fairmont Hotel, a play at the Curran Theater, strolling hand-in-hand along Ocean Beach, or wandering through the Marina, Telegraph Hill, and Chinatown.

Nonie then said, "Johnny, your mother told me those days with Angelo were exhilarating and fun. He was exactly what she needed to help free her from the pain of a failed marriage. She was also pleasantly surprised at how easily she melded into the white mainstream when she was with Angelo. As a girl, she had occasionally fantasized that she was colorless, and with Angelo it seemed that she actually was. She said it was a truly emancipating experience."

As for Angelo, he had obviously fallen in love with my mother. As my aunt related the story to me, my mother and Angelo were sitting on a park bench near the Bay, watching the construction of the Golden Gate Bridge, when he told her he loved her and wanted to marry her. They had known each other for three months.

"Eulalie told me she adored Angelo for who he was and for introducing her to a world devoid of the stultifying trappings of blackness in America, but was that enough to build a marriage on? The moment he proposed, your mother said she felt the answer to her own question was a qualified yes. Unfortunately, her decision was far more complicated. She had a two-year-old son to rear, a son she loved and would never give up. Even before she'd met Angelo, she'd had misgivings that taking you away from your father and the secure Martin household might have been a terrible mistake.

*Mama Peachey & daughter, Eulalie in Berkeley*

"Early on, it was apparent to your grandmother and Maudell, and even to me, as young as I was, that Eulalie felt some guilt about severing so many of your roots. She didn't want to compound the problem by getting into an interracial marriage, which might subject you to future rejection and pain.

"And there was more," Nonie told me with a sigh. "The flame of her love for John Martin had not been completely extinguished. It flickered in her heart still, particularly at night as she lay in bed alone waiting for sleep.

"Your mother said it was several minutes before she responded to Angelo. She looked at the waters of the Bay lapping against the rocks of the shoreline, her throat constricted, her eyes filled with tears. She felt his arm around her shoulders, gently pulling her toward him. She didn't resist, but rather allowed her cheek to rest for a few seconds against his soft wool-sweatered chest. Then Eulalie told Angelo why she couldn't marry him.

"Johnny, when your Mama Peachey and I heard the story of your mother's breakup with Angelo Monti, I cried like a baby. Of course, I had just turned eighteen, and I was young and impressionable, but at the time I thought it was the saddest thing I had ever heard in my life."

I asked Nonie about Mama Peachey's reaction to my mother's breakup with Angelo Monti. I thought the unhappy affair must have brought back images and emotions from her past. And I was right.

"Oh, Johnny, let me tell you. Mama was dead set against Eulalie having anything to do with Angelo Monti from the very beginning, and the weird part is, she seemed to like him personally. It's strange, given Mama's racial background, but she had a problem with his being white.

"She would repeatedly say, 'There's nothing but trouble for you in that relationship, Eulalie.' Then she would add, 'Besides, JohnnyBoy is a dead giveaway that you're part Negro, unless you tell people he's adopted, and that would be an awful thing to do. You can't drag that poor, sweet child through a life where he's going to be treated like a nigger every day he breathes. I didn't raise you to treat a child like that.'

"Mama started that refrain when your mother and Angelo first met and she didn't stop singing it until they broke-up. I think that in you she saw herself as a child again, except life would have been even more difficult for you because of your brown skin. So, yes, your Mama Peachey definitely played her hand, and it was a compelling one. But, you know, I don't believe your mother needed Mama's counsel to decide the way she did. You meant far too much to her for her to have ignored what was best for you."

I, too, was struck by the sadness inherent in the story of my mother's breakup with her Italian boyfriend, and not only because of the tragedy of their unfulfilled romance. I thought of the absurdity of a world in which major life decisions are often predicated on the ultra-superficial human distinction called race: a distinction which is made even more ridiculous in the case of my Peachey family's racial hybridity.

I was equally touched by my grandmother's apparent concern for me, and I was sure Nonie didn't exaggerate it. Mama Peachey and I always had a special affinity for each other. For a year and a half she had lovingly ministered to my toddler needs. And later, for over seven years, I lived only a short block away from her Dohr Street home. During my childhood we did a thousand small but fulfilling things together. No, I was not surprised that Mama Peachey had looked out for my interests in the way that Nonie described.

As I thought about Nonie's story, I wondered why my mother never told me about her ill-fated romance with Angelo Monti. In fits of anger she usually couldn't resist bludgeoning me with sacrifices she had made on my behalf, and the Angelo Monti story would have been a pretty good weapon. But to her everlasting credit, she didn't do that, and it surprises me still.

# Chapter 13

# New Beginnings and
# Different Perspectives

In an effort to understand when my mother's relationship with Lawrence Jared Haynes began, I asked Nonie if there had been some degree of overlap between Angelo and Larry. I was not questioning my mother's morals, but Nonie's initial response went directly to that issue.

"Why, Johnny, I'm surprised you would think that about your mother," she chided.

My mother and her sisters had a very proper Victorian notion of themselves, although with Nonie and Maudell I sometimes thought it was tongue-in-cheek.

"As I recall, Eulalie was totally focused on Angelo during their brief romance. She knew Larry, of course, because he was part of Maudell's group of friends. He used to come to our house often, but during the time Angelo and Eulalie were an item, Larry spent far less time with your mother than he did playing with you, and you adored him.

"I remember times when Larry would get permission from Eulalie to take you out for ice cream or rides in his car. Sometimes your mother would go along, but more often it was just you and Larry. Then, when Angelo was no longer in the picture, it became the three of you. Larry was genuinely fond of you, but he was also smart enough to know he could get to Eulalie through you."

Larry Haynes did emerge from the pack of amorous young colored men to become Eulalie's primary suitor and, later her second husband, and my stepfather. My first memories of a father are of Larry, and I called him Daddy.

Lawrence Haynes was born and reared in Cheyenne, Wyoming. He was an intelligent, handsome, medium brown-skinned man, slightly under six feet tall, with a quick easy smile, straight black hair befitting his part Blackfoot Indian heritage, and a lifelong penchant for pretty mulatto women. He was to become a loving, devoted, long suffering husband, and a good father.

When Larry was sixteen, the death of his mother, Pearl, drastically altered the course of his life. Instead of enrolling as a pre-med undergraduate at the University of Colorado, as he and his mother had long planned, Larry spent an unfocused, unproductive year as a freshman at the University of Nebraska before dropping out of college and living aimlessly for a short time in Omaha.

He moved to California in the late 1920s, planning to remain in the Bay Area for only a short time before moving on to Honolulu to work for Nollie Smith, a cousin who was achieving prominence in Hawaii business and government. Like his abortive college career, Larry let this promise of a tremendous opportunity for a successful and lucrative future slip away.

After a year he decided to remain in Oakland where his father and Uncle Wayne now lived and where he was having a great deal of fun with a free-swinging group of young people he'd met, including a contingent of very pretty mulatto women.

Larry was not, however, lacking in ambition. He enrolled in the San Francisco College of Mortuary Science and worked as an apprentice in an Oakland mortuary, all the while maintaining a full-time job in the supply department of the Pacific Fire Rating Bureau in San Francisco. Unfortunately, he didn't complete his mortuary studies, although he periodically worked over the years as an unlicensed embalmer and was known in the trade as a skilled craftsman.

When Mother and I first arrived in Berkeley, Larry Haynes was engaged to marry his long-time girl friend, Onita Crawford, a stunning, green-eyed woman of Cherokee Indian and white-black ancestry. Onita was well educated, gentle, articulate, and devoted to Larry Haynes. She was as fetching a beauty as my mother, with considerably less baggage. Nevertheless, Larry fell in love with Eulalie shortly after Maudell introduced him to her "visiting, married sister from Houston."

Eulalie Peachey Martin and Lawrence Jared Haynes were married on January 1, 1935, exactly sixteen months after she left Houston and her first husband for what was ostensibly a one-month vacation in Berkeley. Larry had won his prized mulatto woman, and Eulalie had found a superb stepfather for JohnnyBoy. He was twenty-seven, she was twenty-six, and I was three.

I have only one memory of our first days together as a family. It's always the same. I can see a softly inclined hill in San Francisco, just steep enough for me to gain good momentum while coasting down the sidewalk in my toy car with my new daddy walking rapidly beside me. Once, twice, three times I descend the hill laughing happily as the cold January wind sweeps across my face, reddening my cheeks, and bringing water to my eyes. Then Daddy is holding my small fingers in one of his large hands, and my car in the other, as we climb the steps to the door of an apartment, and the dreamlike memory fades into blankness.

Our first house was a small, four-room rented cottage on Harper Street in Berkeley. The earliest real memories I have of my life are of things that happened in that small house, like the evening in June 1936 when Mother and Daddy allowed me to stay up past my 7:30 bedtime, a thrillingly rare event for a four-year-old. The extraordinary occasion was the radio broadcast of a major boxing event; a fight with special meaning for colored folks throughout the country because of the participation of one of the fighters: a dignified, soft-spoken, young Negro from Detroit, Michigan, named Joseph Louis Barrow.

In June 1936, Joe Louis was undefeated in twenty-seven professional fights and seemed destined to become the first black heavyweight champion of the world since the controversial Jack Johnson lost the title in 1915. Joe Louis' ring victories, golden future, and quiet dignity made him an idol among Negroes, and gave hope to tens of thousands that they too might someday shed the heavy chains of racism and poverty.

I remember that I wore a brown fleece robe over my pajamas that night. I asked Mother if I could take the robe off while I played with building blocks and soldiers in the middle of the living room floor, but she said no, because I might get chilled. Then Daddy told me that Joe Louis was wearing a robe as he walked down the aisle to the boxing ring. With that surprising knowledge, I no longer wanted to shed my robe.

That long ago evening which began with such excitement ended disastrously, as our hero, Joe Louis, suffered his first loss in the ring. The dejection I took to bed with me that night was the same sadness I sensed in my mother and stepfather; a sadness, I learned later, that affected black people across the entire nation.

My new daddy taught me how to fight. He told me it was important that I fight back whenever another kid abused me. He said it was downright cowardly for me to run home crying every time somebody started pushing me around.

"I know it's not your fault that you can't fight," Daddy said. "Poor kid, you've been surrounded by women too long. Well that's changed now. A boy needs a real man in his life to become a man himself, otherwise he might just become a sissy, or a punk.

"Johnny, there are two things I want you to always remember to do. Defend yourself, and always tell me the truth. Daddy promises not to spank you if you tell me the truth and if you stand tall and fight back when another kid attacks you, or calls you nigger. Do you understand, Son?"

"Yes, Daddy, but suppose the other person is a girl? Mother said I shouldn't hit girls."

"Well, now, your mother's mostly right, Johnny, 'cause good girls don't hit boys. But if a girl hits you, she's definitely not a good girl, and you ought to hit her back. So my advice to you is to knock her on her ass, like you would anyone else who hits you."

"Okay, Daddy," I said, hoping I'd never encounter a bad girl, nor, for that matter, too many free-swinging boys. Of course, I didn't say that to Daddy, since I wanted to please him and not have him think of me as a sissy.

Daddy brought me boxing gloves and every night after he came home from work we boxed with the gloves or in openhanded combat. I was surprised at how much fun it was learning to fight. Daddy taught me how to balance my weight on the balls of my feet, how to hold my hands high, with my right fist cocked and held a few inches from my jaw, and my left, lower on the opposite side of my body, ready to attack with a knuckles-up jab to my opponent's face. It was the classic Joe Louis stance.

Daddy was a good and thorough instructor, and he praised me generously when I showed progress. When I learned to feint with a right hand lead and quickly throw a double left hook to the head, I remember he hugged me, patted my head, and said I was a terrific kid.

Mother usually remained in the background while Daddy was indoctrinating me in the manly art of self-defense. I don't ever recall my mother giving her blessing to fisticuffs training, nor do I remember her voicing an objection. I suspect, from the way things unfolded, that my parents had reached an understanding, and manhood training was Daddy's domain. Nevertheless, I always had a sense of my mother hovering in the background, watching, monitoring, assessing.

*John Jr. & mother, Eulalie*

I eventually learned enough to defend myself on the streets and playgrounds of South Berkeley and was respected among my peers as a kid who could and would fight if necessary. The most important thing to me, however, was winning Daddy's love and approval and that made defending myself essential.

One night when I was about eight years old, I finished saying my prayers, kissed Mother and Daddy good night and got in bed. In the dark I pulled the covers up under my chin, closed my eyes tightly and visualized Jesus delivering the Sermon on the Mount. "God," I prayed, "in addition to blessing my relatives and friends, caring for the poorest of the poor, and giving me the strength to be a good boy, please also give me the strength and the courage tomorrow to face up to that bully Frankie Moore, and to kick his ass if he continues to fuck with me. Thank you, Lord."

After school the following day I did indeed kick Frankie Moore's ass. I hit Frankie with a perfectly timed overhand right to the nose (only after he had fucked with me, of course) and his blood spurted everywhere. I was elated. I had successfully melded the lessons of my mother, who had taught me to trust in prayer, and of my stepfather, who had taught me to trust in a hard right to my opponent's nose.

Daddy had seen me demolish Frankie Moore from our front porch. Minutes later he held me so tightly in his arms I couldn't breathe. "That's my boy, that's my boy," he kept repeating, occasionally varying his pitch and intonation until it began to sound like a college victory song. I was deliriously happy Daddy was pleased with me. I felt loved by him.

When he finally let me go, I spotted my mother through our open bathroom door. She was tenderly washing Frankie Moore's face and talking to him so softly I couldn't hear what she was saying. When I saw my mother ministering to Frankie, I began to feel guilty over having hurt him and I wondered if Mother was angry with me for fighting. Just then, as if she had heard my thoughts, she turned and looked at me with a smile that said she wasn't angry. A few minutes later, Mother, with one arm around Frankie's shoulder and the other around mine, told us to shake hands, which we did.

Although my exhilaration over the victory was now tinged with regret, I still didn't tell Frankie I was sorry and the looks we exchanged made it clear that the tables had turned. From now on I was his master on the street.

Daddy clapped Frankie on his back and said, "You'll be fine, Tiger. You stood and fought like a man. It's no shame to get beaten by a better man, just as long as you stand and fight."

For years afterward, Daddy talked about my conquest of Frankie Moore in the most glowing terms to anyone who would listen.

During my childhood it was customary for parents not to disagree with each other in the presence of the children. Eulalie and Larry generally adhered to that custom. Nevertheless I occasionally overheard conversations that weren't meant for my ears. One such conversation between my parents which I overhead went something like this:

Mother: "Lawrence, I don't want my child to become a thug."

Daddy: "Oh, come on, Honey, I'm teachin' the boy to defend himself, that's all. Johnny's gotta learn to protect himself or he'll become a sissy, and the next thing we know, some degenerate kid will have him in the bushes with his pants down corn-holing him."

Mother: "Corn-holing? What does that mean?"

"Oh, you know. Doin' it to someone in the butt."

Mother: "Lawrence, that's absolutely disgusting."

Daddy: "Listen, I'm tellin' you, it happens."

Mother: "Well, I'm not aware of it happening to boys I grew up with, and many of them were nice kids who didn't go around fighting."

Daddy: "Different place, different time. Besides, Honey, what you don't know about the things that happened to the boys you grew up with would probably fill a book. I'm only trying to give our son tools to protect himself from the real dangers of the street."

Although she never said so to me, I guess my mother was, at best, ambivalent over the prospect of her JohnnyBoy becoming a well-oiled fighting machine. I know she loathed the possibility of my becoming a street-fighting bully, but I guess she was also frightened by the notion of my getting hurt because I couldn't defend myself.

My mother saw in me many of the positive traits of my father, John Martin: intelligence, sensitivity, obedience, love of parents -- and she rarely missed an opportunity to say so. She also believed my biological father was absent when street-fighting genes were dispensed, so if father and son were alike, my inherited love of peace would automatically influence the extent to which I absorbed Daddy's violence training.

She therefore continued to tolerate her second husband's manly training of her first husband's son, who without such training might have become a wimp, and possibly worse.

Daddy was also an every-boy-should-have-a-dog kinda guy, but Mother was not particularly fond of dogs. Nevertheless, Mother did allow me to have two dogs, albeit briefly, when I was growing up. Both were German shepherds, Daddy's favorite breed. The second of my two dogs was named Eric. He was about three years old when Daddy brought him home one Saturday afternoon. Eric could shake hands and roll over on his back on command. Neat.

One day, Eric chased my mother up the back stairs of our house because she dared to grab my arm and reprimand me in front of him. The very next day Eric was gone; our friendship terminated by his lifetime banishment from our family. I missed him and wished he'd had the sense not to chase Mother up those stairs.

Pal, my first dog, was a gift from Daddy on my fourth birthday. He lasted only three months before he mysteriously disappeared. I was told he was stolen, and that may have been true since Pal and my mother seemed to be bonding at the time of his disappearance. Still, snippets of conversation I overheard prior to Pal's "theft" may also have had some bearing on the case.

My mother said, "Lawrence, I am not interested in cleaning up dog shit every day."

And Daddy replied, "Then don't."

To which my mother said, "Believe me, my dear, I don't intend to."

Several weeks after Pal left us, Mother and Daddy told me we'd probably never see him again. Up until then, I had remained hopeful we would find him. I cried especially long and hard the day hope died.

Pal's empty house remained in our backyard and my friend, George Dean, and I used it to play house with Julie, a little girl who lived across the street. One day Julie volunteered to take the place of my missing Pal. Since dogs don't wear underwear, she lowered her panties and crawled head first into Pal's old house, leaving only her bare butt protruding from the entry.

"You can pat it like you used to pat Pal," she said.

Julie, who was a worldly six at the time, assigned a cheek to each of us with instructions to gently rub, which we did dutifully while eating

Popsicles. We offered to save Julie's Popsicle until she exited the doghouse, but she preferred to eat it while George and I rubbed. Unfortunately, Julie's butt was devoid of hair and it simply didn't feel like Pal.

During the first four years of Mother and Daddy's married life, we went on three camping vacations that I can remember. Daddy loved to camp out, and he owned a tent and lots of camping equipment, including a cook stove, cots, chairs, and other odds and ends. Next to extended family Christmases at Mama Peachey's house, camping was, for a short time, my favorite family activity. Mother, however, simply did not share the enthusiasm Daddy and I felt for the Great Outdoors.

I remember overhearing my mother say, "Lawrence, I'm so sorry. I just can't deal with the bugs, the dirt, and not being able to take a warm bath."

To which Daddy replied, "I know. Don't feel badly. You've been a good scout, and you've really tried. It's my fault for not taking you to the mountains, or to a beautiful pine forest, or to a meadow over lookin' the ocean. I think those are places where you might really enjoy campin'. We could even try stayin' in a cabin."

"I don't know, Lawrence, maybe staying in a cabin would make a difference. I know how much you love the outdoors, and I hate spoiling your fun. Maybe you and Johnny could go camping without me sometime. He loves camping with you."

"I know he does, but it wouldn't be the same for me without you, Eulalie. Please don't feel like you're spoilin' my fun, 'cause bein' with you means more to me than anything else. We'll figure somethin' out."

They figured it out by completely giving up camping shortly after my brother, Lawrence II, was born in 1939.

I'm convinced that my stepfather never lost his love for the great outdoors, however; an ardor that flowed from his Wyoming childhood and his Blackfoot Indian heritage. He frequently talked of hunting and fishing and traipsing through the woods on old Indian trails. A faraway look would come over his face as he remembered campfires and sleeping under the stars and the loyalty and bravery of his dog, Wolf, and the fearlessness of his Uncle Wayne, the expert horseman and cowboy.

Given the time, money, and opportunity, I imagine my stepfather's ideal life as an adult would likely have included many days and nights living off the land. He would have loved exploring one-time Native American byways of mountain, forest, plain and shore, preferably with the woman he loved.

As for my mother, I visualize her being truly happy in Paris or Copenhagen or Rome or Madrid. She would have been in her element living in first class hotels or seaside villas, eating in the best restaurants, visiting museums and historical sites, attending the latest shows and dancing in chic clubs till dawn. But these were places she would never see and things she would never do, given the circumstances of her life and the narrow racial box to which she had been assigned. In fact, the likelihood is that Eulalie never even came close to imagining such a life for herself; her dreams stunted by the realities of her Southern mulatto-Negro origins.

What she talked about most often instead, was the provincial life she and my father enjoyed during their brief marriage. Her eyes would close with fond memories as she spoke of friendships with young couples they had known since childhood, parties, dances, picnics, drives to Galveston. My mother consistently longed for, cherished and romanticized a life that was gone forever.

# CHAPTER 14

# THE HOUSTON VISIT

In the summer of 1939, my mother, Little Larry and I traveled by train to Houston. Mother packed a steamer trunk and two suitcases with far more clothes than we would need for a three-week vacation. We went to visit my mother's sisters, Louise and Bessie, their families, and the Martins.

I'm sure my stepfather had some misgivings about being separated from his family for three weeks but, as I recall, he seemed outwardly pleased that my mother had the opportunity to visit her sisters. The trip was made possible by the largess of my Grandpa Martin, who sent us round-trip railroad passes.

Daddy had lived with Mother long enough to know how very close the members of the Peachey family were to one another. Aside from the good times Eulalie shared with her husband and son, Daddy knew she was happiest when she was around her sisters and Mama Peachey in Berkeley. Still, I'm sure he also recalled that his wife's trip from Houston to Berkeley, six years earlier, had also been billed as a vacation but had resulted in a permanent relocation and divorce.

He did know that his wife's ex-husband was finally engaged to marry, and he must have considered that a good omen. He may have also thought about his own engagement to Onita, abruptly brought to an end by my mother's arrival in Berkeley. I wonder if it occurred to him that history sometimes had a way of repeating itself.

Daddy drove us to the Southern Pacific train station at the foot of University Avenue on a cloudy, windy morning in August. He brought our luggage onto the train and made us comfortable in two, facing coach seats. We waved our goodbyes through the coach window as Daddy stood on the station platform, waving back.

The caring look Daddy beamed up to us, and Mother whispering I love you with her face pressed to the train window, her eyes fixed on her husband, gave me such a warm feeling. I smiled broadly from inner delight. They were the only parents I wanted and I was happiest when they showed signs of loving each other, which was often but not always.

In 1939 my "real father," as Mother insisted on calling him, had given up pharmacy as a career and started teaching chemistry and biology at Phyllis Wheatley High School in Houston. The school was located near the home of Aunt Louise, who kept tabs on my father's doings and regularly reported her findings to my mother. Louise's son, Bill, and Aunt Bessie's daughter, June, attended Phyllis Wheatley High and both had been in classes my father taught.

Erma Johnson, my father's very beautiful mulatto sweetheart, lived a few houses away from Aunt Louise. With all these sources of information, Louise was well-stocked with the latest news regarding John Martin, which she knew her sister Eulalie was ever anxious to hear.

My paternal grandparents also wrote to my mother about their son's courtship of Erma Johnson. They disliked Erma, primarily because she was a divorcee and this offended their Catholic sensibilities. But Erma was also a strong, independent woman, candid, outspoken, and contentious when it suited her, the antithesis of what my grandparents considered the ideal girl.

What they expected my mother to do about the John-Erma relationship was never clear to me. After all, their son and former daughter-in-law had been divorced for six years. Eulalie also had a six-month-old son by the man she had been married to for the past four years. Nevertheless, I suspect that in some compartment of the thoroughly Catholic minds of my grandparents, John and Eulalie were still husband and wife, and Erma Johnson was a worldly, free-spirited interloper of dubious character and background.

*Erma Johnson Martin*

One of the first things my mother did after we settled in at Aunt Louise's was to arrange a private meeting with Erma Johnson. I suspect she read the reports of her sister and former in-laws with something more than passing interest.

Once, when my mother and I were reminiscing on that 1939 Houston vacation, she casually mentioned that she had given Erma "a few tips" on how to deal with the Martins as in-laws. I never pressed her for details. Several decades later, Erma described that meeting with my mother as a "not unfriendly, frank exchange of views."

I remember Erma relaxing on a couch in her family room, a half-smoked cigarette between her fingers and a thoughtful, reflective smile on her lovely cafe au lait colored face as she gave me the details of her long-ago meeting with my mother.

"Eulalie told me John's great failing as a man was his inability to stand up to his parents when it mattered. Not only had he let her and his son drift out of his life, but he had also abandoned his college sweetheart, a girl named Lena Williams, because that was what his folks wanted."

I told Erma that I had heard the bare outlines of the Lena Williams episode.

"Did you know your father got Lena pregnant in their first and only sexual encounter?" Erma asked me.

"No, I didn't know that," I said with genuine shock and surprise.

"Well, that's the gospel truth. But instead of marryin' the girl like he wanted to do, he abandoned the poor thing 'cause his parents told him that's what they wanted him to do. Eulalie reminded me of that dark chapter in your father's life, as well as his failure to accept either of the two research opportunities offered to him on the East Coast, because his parents disapproved.

"I told your mother that these were the mistakes of a very young man who was not only devoted to his parents, but felt he owed them for all they had done for him. Eulalie agreed with me, but said John continued to manifest those weak, dependent tendencies during the course of their marriage.

"She also told me straight out that Mr. and Mrs. Martin didn't like me and they weren't shy about sayin' so to other people. Now, in spite of the fact I knew they didn't like me and I wasn't so sure about John's assurances that they would come around, I didn't know they had shared their negative opinions of me with other people, including my fiancé's ex-wife. That made me mad, not at Eulalie, but at your grandparents.

"When your mother saw I was stung by that bit of intelligence she quickly followed up by describing how the Martins' interference in her married life drove her to a nervous breakdown. 'They liked me,' she said, 'so you can imagine what your life will be like as their unwanted daughter-in-law.'

"Johnny, I knew Eulalie had a point and she certainly made it effectively, but I loved your father and I wasn't going to let his parents, his ex-wife, or anyone else dissuade me from marrying him. I told that to Eulalie. I told her that I was older, more experienced, and emotionally stronger than she was during her marriage to John. I told her I could deal with whatever shit the elder Martins threw my way. I didn't intend to marry John's parents, I said, but I did intend to marry John.

"You know, after that meeting with Eulalie, I was more determined than ever to do what my heart told me to do and marry your father, although I must confess I was more than a little shaken by our conversation. You see, I suddenly realized that Eulalie may have still been in love with John and, believe me, that was a big time shock."

I'm convinced my mother reveled in the fact that the Martins preferred her to Erma. I remember Grandma and Grandpa Martin enthusiastically welcoming my mother into their home during that 1939 visit. They greeted her like she had returned home from an extended vacation. They repeatedly hugged her and every time they looked at her, their faces were lit with approving smiles.

I don't remember any of the words that passed between my mother and her former in-laws, but even as a seven-year-old I was struck by the fact all three cried the first time my mother brought me to their house, and I couldn't understand why.

Excluding the twenty-one months of their marriage following my birth, there was only one time in my entire life that my mother, father, and I were alone together. It was a Sunday afternoon, three months before my eighth birthday. They were in the front seat of Dad's (as I called him in later years) automobile and I was in the back.

I don't remember the beginning or ending details of the short time the three of us were together that day. I do remember I was feeling uncomfortable dressed in my best Sunday clothes sitting in my father's car. I wanted to be elsewhere, playing with my cousin Irwin, Aunt Bessie's son.

My mother and father spoke to each other in the soft, easy cadences of old friends as we drove through parts of the city. At one point, my father stopped the car next to a park, and bought me an ice cream sandwich from a park vendor while he and Mother continued to talk in the front seat of the car, their voices slightly more audible with the engine turned off. I could have listened to their conversation had I been interested, but I wasn't. They may have even discussed getting back together as husband and wife that day for all I know.

It was only as a young adult that I began to appreciate the uniqueness of those minutes in which the three of us shared the same space for the only time in my memory. Since that summer afternoon in 1939, I've often wondered what my life would have been like had my mother and father never divorced.

Two days after that Sunday drive with my father, Mother, Little Larry and I boarded a Southern Pacific train and returned to Berkeley. As far as I could tell, my mother's only regret in leaving Houston was being separated again from Louise and Bessie. Several weeks after we arrived in Berkeley, Aunt Louise telephoned Mother with the news that my father and Erma Johnson had married.

## Chapter 15

# The Periodic Drinker

To some extent, I may have begun to see my mother's drinking as an entrenched family problem in the early 1940s, but I also lived with the hope that her last drink was, indeed, her last. I've never forgotten the scary childhood memories of drinking-related arguments and fights between my mother and stepfather. But as a child I tended to see each of those nightmarish episodes as unconnected to a continuous pattern of behavior.

Mother's drinking was periodic and for many years there were extended periods of sobriety between her brief bouts with the bottle. I'm sure her periodic drinking pattern led her family to believe that she could stop permanently if she really wanted to. That was certainly what I believed.

Mother evidently didn't drink as a youth or during her young adult life in Houston. It was Aunt Bessie who told me my mother started drinking after she came to California in 1933.

"She became part of Maudell's group of friends and, honey, that was a fast crowd. Larry was part of that group. That's how Eulalie met him. I know for a fact that Eulalie didn't drink when she lived in Houston, either before or during her marriage to John. I was there and I saw my sister almost daily during that time."

My father said basically the same thing. "Eulalie didn't drink during the entire time we were together," he told me. "She simply didn't like alcohol. And you know, Son, in those days not drinking was central to what was considered a proper ladylike image, and that image was important to your mother."

My father and Aunt Bessie were both pretty convincing. In addition, my stepfather repeatedly confirmed what Aunt Bessie told me about the heavy drinking tendencies of the social set he and Aunt Maudell belonged to at the time my mother arrived on the scene. Daddy liked to expound on a drinking philosophy he, Aunt Maudell and others shared in the 1930s.

The key to drinking, according to Daddy, was "being able to hold your liquor." By that he meant not having a drastic personality change which resulted in the drinker getting mean, or sloppy, or weepy, or maudlin, or sick, or passing-out.

Daddy was fond of saying, "If you can't hold your liquor, you shouldn't drink. It doesn't matter how much you drink, just as long as you can hold your liquor." This was my stepfather's drinking code when he met and married my mother.

Daddy drank straight shots of 100% Old Grand Dad whiskey in those early days. "This is a real man's drink," he would say. "If you're going to drink, you might as well drink the best."

In the beginning, my mother couldn't drink large quantities of any alcoholic beverage, but one drink was enough to alter her personality. And two drinks could transform her into an excessively talkative, often paranoid, sometimes mean and foul-mouthed drunk who idolized a past life she had impulsively given up.

As Daddy often said with a shake of his head, "Your mother definitely can't hold her liquor."

Interestingly, this was not the case with Brother, Maudell and Nonie. They drank liberally and were known for being able to "drink with the best of 'em."

Not all of the Peacheys were drinkers, but alcohol was generally available at family gatherings. The decibel level usually intensified as family members drank, but it seems only Eulalie became a dramatically different person. I believe it was this personality change while drinking that resulted in her siblings' distancing themselves from her.

During my childhood and adolescence, I cherished my mother's periods of sobriety. I remember a time she went over a year without a drink. There were even times during my preadolescence when Mother would bake a Christmas fruitcake in October, wrap it in a gauze-like cloth and periodically feed it with small amounts of wine or whiskey for two months, but never drink a drop herself.

Since the quantity of liquor she consumed in the early days of her periodic habit was so small, she usually didn't have classic hangovers. But she almost always seemed to me to project an aura of sadness and shame the day after a drinking episode. I could see it in her eyes and the slowness of her step as she moved around the house performing her daily chores.

When the veil of sadness lifted and my mother had pulled herself out of the depths of her despair, our home became a happy place. My stepfather's engaging smile returned and, with it, a loving gentleness toward his sober wife. There were phone calls and visits from my grandmother and aunts and Mother's public persona re-emerged.

When she wasn't drinking, Mother might meet with the principal of my school in her role as president of the Parent Teachers Association, or visit one of my classrooms in her reoccurring capacity as homeroom parent, or attend choir practice at the Fifteenth Street African Methodist Episcopal Church, or enthusiastically shop for her family in local food markets.

My chest would swell with pride when she appeared at my schools. She was always completely sober on those occasions. I loved watching the reaction of white teachers, administrators, and other parents when they had face-to-face contact with her.

What I enjoyed most was the momentary embarrassment of whites when they realized for the first time that Mother and I were connected. It was as if they expected some handkerchief-headed Aunt Jemimah to be my mother and, instead got this near-white apparition. Generally, these were friendly encounters between Mother and others. There were, however, other situations which were decidedly confrontational. Mother's visit with my eighth grade Spanish teacher was one of those.

Miss Jarwelski was the only blatantly racist teacher I remember encountering as a student in the Berkeley public school system. There were three African American students in her class. Jarwelski assigned all three of us seats in the back of the classroom, while allowing the remainder of the students to sit wherever they chose. She never called on me or the other two black kids when we raised our hands to answer questions. Yet she frequently called on us when we failed to raise our hands. Jarwelski was into derision and embarrassment in the crudest of ways, laughing at our mistakes and mispronunciations during oral recitations and cruelly demeaning us in front of our classmates.

"Why are you people so dense? I can't understand why any one of the three of you enrolled in this class. None of you have an aptitude for learning Spanish and your presence in this classroom is a drag on the learning of other students."

Until I reached high school and lived with my father for a year in racially segregated Houston, I generally believed racism directed at me was a mistake. It wasn't that I didn't believe blacks weren't discriminated against, but when I was the victim my first reaction was that the victimizer had mistakenly singled me out. Perhaps this was simply a normal youthful reaction to the irrationality of racism, but it probably also related to my being reared in a mulatto environment.

In any event, I was thoroughly humiliated by Miss Jarwelski's invidious treatment. At the same time, I had difficulty believing it was happening to me. For a time I said nothing to my mother. But the mean, discriminatory treatment was relentless and I received a D grade in Spanish for the first report period.

That D in Spanish forced me to share the details of my humiliation with Mother. When I finished my story, tears welled in my eyes despite my best effort to hold them back. My mother cradled my head below her shoulder, and said, "I'm so very sorry this happened to you, my son. You should have told me the minute that bitch started treating you like a nigger. I would have put a stop to it immediately. Why didn't you tell me sooner?"

"I guess I thought it would stop. I was so ashamed, and I don't think I'm very good at Spanish anyway. I just thought she was kidding around at first, and I expected her to stop acting like that."

"Well, let this be a lesson to you. Bigots don't stop that kind of behavior on their own because they're basically ignorant, mean-spirited people and they don't see any difference between you and some common Negro. They must be taught that you are different, and under no circumstances are you to be treated in a racist manner. Tomorrow I'll be in Miss Jarwelski's classroom and I guarantee you she won't treat you like a nigger again, not ever."

The very next day my mother entered Miss Jarwelski's room a few minutes before class began. I had taken my seat early so I wouldn't miss my mother's arrival. Jarwelski was writing Spanish grammar on the blackboard when my mother came in.

Mother was wearing the navy blue gabardine suit she wore on very special occasions, with matching high-heeled shoes, a pearl necklace and a wide brimmed cream-colored hat, which partially hid her lowered face. She waited until she was practically nose-to-nose with Jarwelski, raised her head and revealed the full beauty of her face to the startled Spanish teacher.

"I'm Mrs. Haynes, John Martin's mother, and I'm here to confront the unacceptable bigoted behavior you've directed at my son."

Whenever racism touched her children, Mother didn't mince words. She went directly into an attack mode.

"I..I don't understand," the startled teacher stammered. She looked at my mother then at me, back and forth several times, her mouth agape, her head shaking in disbelief.

Mother relentlessly pressed on, "What is it you don't understand? I said I am Mrs. Haynes, John Martin's mother, and our subject today is your racist treatment of my son. Do you have problems with the English language, Miss Jar-wel-ski?"

My mother pointed at me and asked me to stand. "Look at him. He's not a nigger and if you continue to treat him as such, I'll not only have you fired, but I'll make your life a living hell. I want him moved to the front of this room before I leave and I want him treated with kindness and respect by you on a daily basis. Teach him and don't you dare humiliate him. Do you understand me now, Miss Jar-wel-ski?"

Before my mother left the classroom, Miss Jarwelski had claimed she wasn't a racist, apologized for unintentionally hurting my feelings, apologized for any misunderstanding of her intentions toward me, apologized for any upset she had caused my mother, moved me to the front of the room, and promised to work extra hard with me to ensure my success in Spanish. She also managed to compliment my mother and unwittingly insult me in the same breath when she gushed how astounded she was to see that John's mother was so beautiful.

# CHAPTER 16

# THE MULATTO IMPACT

I've always psychologically identified as African American and all my mulatto relatives do, as well. Nevertheless, the white, black, and Seminole Indian heritage of the mulatto Peacheys also gave me a certain sense of uniqueness. By the time I became intellectually aware that a very large cross section of Negro America had some White and/or Indian admixture, the notion of my own distinctiveness had already been ingrained.

My mother's physical beauty and that of my grandmother and five aunts was a definite source of pride for me. It wasn't something I bragged or even talked about outside the confines of the family but I wore it like a badge of honor at the front of my psyche.

Why was the physical beauty of the Peachey women so important to me and to other members of our family? First, it approximated the European standard of beauty, the prevailing benchmark in Western society. Second, my mulatto heritage allowed me to experience a small degree of psychological separation from darker-hued blacks in our anti-black society. In effect, the horrendous burden of American racism has often been somewhat heavier on the backs of my darker-skinned brethren than it has been on mine -- a carry over from slavery, when most of the field hands were black and many of the house servants were brown or beige or cream colored.

There really is no such thing as a genetically monolithic black race in America, white supremacist ideology and oversimplified racial labeling notwithstanding. The differences in skin color, facial features and hair texture between members of my family and many other Negroes were readily apparent to me early on. The stories the adults in my family told in the sanctuary of the home often described their distinct, everyday experiences as mulattoes.

So the seeds of difference were planted in my mind as a very young child. There was Mama Peachey's youthful social metamorphosis from white to black. Then there were the vignettes I heard as a child, which described Mama's encounters with racist white strangers who initiated conversations with her based on the false assumption that she was white. Even as a child, I was impressed by the way my grandmother handled those encounters. I remember that each of the episodes followed the same pattern: Mama first listening patiently without comment as the stranger spewed forth an array of disgusting racist attitudes toward Negroes and then, with high drama and fiery passion, Mama would state that she herself was a Negro and proceed to scold and demean her companion for harboring racist attitudes. Years later, in reflecting on those particular experiences of my grandmother, I began to see her as an unacknowledged spokesperson in the broad based struggle for racial understanding in America.

There were also the many instances of common, public, social courtesies I saw routinely granted to my mother and grandmother; courtesies just as routinely denied other Negroes with pronounced black visibility. I can never recall an instance when my mother was the object of a public, racial insult. In fact, I do not remember ever hearing stories in which any of my aunts were humiliated in public because they were Negroes. If they had such experiences, they weren't shared with their children.

I was, in a sense, a secondary beneficiary of the subtle social rewards of my mother being mulatto. Nevertheless, I was brown-skinned and visibly Negro, which meant inevitable exposure to the realities of racism in America. Still, the overt racism I experienced as a child was sufficiently infrequent that I did not generally anticipate it, nor was I automatically prepared to combat it.

However, my mother and stepfather were ever vigilant to the possibility of racist behavior being directed at their children. They trained us to overtly reject racism and to strike back whenever it was directed at us personally.

I believe the mulatto equation somehow heightened my parents' sensitivity to possible racial slights aimed at their children. It was as if my parents were not only poised to take on whites who treated their children in a racist manner, but their outrage seemed to be compounded because bigots did not distinguish between us and other Negroes.

Both attitudes were demonstrated in the episode involving Mother and Miss Jarwelski. The gist of Mother's message to me before she confronted Miss Jarwelski was twofold: First, I must never ignore bigotry. Second, I must take direct action against it. "Otherwise bigots won't change their behavior."

There is no doubt in my mind that Mother's being mulatto combined with her good looks had as much impact the day she confronted Miss Jarwelski as did her expressed outrage at the teacher's racist behavior and failure to see me as different from my Negro classmates. The result of Mother's presence and message that day extended beyond Miss Jarwelski's changed attitude toward me.

For me, it was an extraordinarily uplifting experience to witness my mother walking resolutely into the classroom and confronting my racist teacher and remains one of the most vivid memories of my youth. I never forgot the messages of pride, anger and refusal to accept racism, it conveyed.

I also remember kids in the class whispering to each other and turning to look at me as Mother savaged Miss Jarwelski. I overheard several girls, including Ellie Monroe (whom I adored but who had not given me a second's notice before mother's appearance) commenting on how very pretty my mother was. Ellie and I became friends following Mother's appearance. She constantly talked about my mother's good looks. It was as if Ellie began to see me through the prism of my mother's prettiness, which was just fine as long as she paid attention to me.

A few days following the Jarwelsky confrontation, I asked my mother why she hadn't spoken out on behalf of the other two black children in the class.

"Both of those kids have mothers," she snapped, "and those women need to get up off their scared black butts and speak up for their own kids. I know it sounds selfish, Johnny, and I feel for those children, but I have no patience with cowardly Negroes."

It wasn't only my mother who forthrightly addressed racial slights against her children. Daddy did so as well, although the mulatto difference didn't seem to be of particular significance in his confrontations. With Daddy, shit was shit and he didn't take it from anybody except Mother, and even with her there were limits. I'll never forget the Saturday afternoon he stopped our car at a red light, jumped out and quickly opened the door of a vehicle parked alongside of us. He grabbed the driver by the lapels of his jacket, pulled him out of the car and punched him in the face so hard the man fell to the ground. Daddy returned to our car by the time the light turned green and slowly drove off. The man my stepfather punched that day had given Daddy the finger and shouted, "Don't drive that piece of crap so slow, nigger."

"Johnny," I remember my stepfather saying, "Your self-respect is one of the most precious things you own and you can't keep it intact if you let others disrespect you. Do you understand?"

I told Daddy that I understood. I neglected to tell him I thought he was the bravest and, next to Joe Louis, the toughest man in the world and I idolized him.

Now, many years later, as the hip-hop music icon Tupac Shakur sings, "That's the way it is, some things will never change," I reflect on the operative anti-racist instructional theme of my mother and stepfather. I am struck by the contrast between Shakur's fatalistic lyrics and the message I got from my parents, which was "fuck the racist way, we'll do our best to make it change."

I was a tall, athletic thirteen-year-old when I accepted a Saturday job shining shoes in Ralph's Barbershop on Market Street in North Oakland. Ralph, a handsome, dark-complexioned black man, was a friend of my stepfather's. He had inherited the barbershop from his father, Ralph, Sr. At the time I went to work for Ralph, the shop had been a thriving neighborhood business for about twenty years.

Ralph let me keep the money I made shining shoes in return for my sweeping the floor around the barber chairs. I also occasionally ran errands to the corner grocery store for Ralph and his co-barber, Jackson. While I never earned more than four or five dollars for an entire Saturday of work, I enjoyed being in the shop. It was fun listening to the funny stories the customers and barbers shared and watching old Joe and Rufus play checkers.

One particularly busy Saturday morning, as I sat on the step of the shoe shine stand focusing on Joe and Rufus match wits across the checkerboard, an elderly white man walked briskly into the shop. I had seen him before and I knew he owned the building in which the shop was located. Ralph and Jackson greeted the landlord politely. He returned their greetings with a scant nod of his head. He seemed not to notice anyone else as he walked toward the back storage room. I noticed that all the talking and laughing in the shop stopped instantly when the old landlord walked through the front door. To me, he had looked so utterly out of place; a grizzled old white man walking through a room full of seated black men.

Several minutes after he entered the storeroom, the landlord emerged holding an armload of lumber. He walked directly to the shoeshine stand, dumped the lumber at my feet and said, "Boy, take these things out to my truck." Neither of us had ever spoken to each other before. In fact, I had only seen him in the neighborhood for the first time the previous week when one of Ralph's customers pointed to him as he emerged from his truck and said, "That ole fart there owns this whole stinkin' block."

Not for a second did the landlord look directly at me. He merely dropped the lumber at my feet, gave me his command, turned around and began walking back to the storeroom.

I remember feeling instantly outraged by that white man's action. I was not some subservient nigger he could disrespect and humiliate. Why couldn't he see that? Did I have to beat the shit out of him to show him I was different, that I wasn't some common nigger field slave?

I shouted at his back, "Who the fuck do you think I am? We're not all the same, motherfucker, and you'd better learn that fast. I'll kick your old white ass before I'll pick up one piece of this shit. Actually I oughta kick it anyway, you son-of-a-bitch."

I took a step toward the old landlord. I could see Jackson out of the corner of my eye turn from his customer and start to move in my direction. I stopped, balled fists at my side glaring at the old man. Jackson stopped, too, but his eyes remained fixed on me.

The landlord was looking at me red-faced, mouth open, startled. He said nothing, but his eyes conveyed fear and pleading. The old man's face told me that I had successfully made my point. The impulse to attack him physically had passed. But I wasn't through. I felt a sense of exhilaration. I suddenly realized that I was on stage. I had an audience and the drama the landlord and I had set in motion needed closing lines.

"Get your white ass back here, pick up this goddamn lumber and get the fuck out of this shop," I ordered. "And the next time you come in here, say hello and show some fuckin' respect. Nobody in here is your nigger, mother fucker, and you better remember that."

The landlord seemed ancient, even feeble, as he walked wordlessly back to where I stood. He bent down, picked up the lumber silently, unsteadily, made his way to the opened front door and outside to his truck.

As he reached the sidewalk, a large black woman crossed his path. Those of us inside the shop could hear her words through the opened door.

"You gon hurt yo'self granfatha," the big black woman exclaimed. "Let me hep you." She reached into his arms and grabbed more than half of the lumber the landlord was carrying. She followed him to his truck and dumped her share of the load into the truck bed.

The landlord bowed his head to the big black woman. "Thank you, ma'am," he said, "you're most kind and thoughtful. May I pay you something for your trouble?" he asked.

"Course not," the big black woman replied. "I done what I did 'cause it was the Christian thing to do. Now you git yo self on home granfatha, or wherever you goin', an' take care."

The big black woman watched the old man as he drove away. Then she turned and looked into the window of the barbershop. She shook her large head disgustedly from side to side and said, "Colored mens ain't gonna lift a finger to hep a soul. I do declare."

Jackson was the first person inside of the shop to speak after the landlord left. "JohnnyBoy, you went too far, son. You shouldn't have threatened the old man, and you know your mama wouldn't approve of the curse words you used. You went a little too far, son."

I looked at Jackson and nodded affirmatively. Still, I was firm in my belief that the landlord had no right to speak to me disrespectfully, dump his lumber at my feet and order me to carry it to his truck.

Ralph seemed to read my mind as he quickly chimed in, "The old man had no right to talk to you that way, Johnny. I know how Eulalie and Larry have raised you, but Larry himself wouldn't have threatened to kick that old man's ass, because it wasn't necessary. Maybe you shoulda stopped before you got there."

Suddenly everyone in the barbershop began to offer opinions at the same time:

"Jackson 'n Ralph is right, that weren't no way to talk to an ole man."

"What you say, that ole man ain't got no business orderin' this young cat around."

"Yeah, he ain't nothin' but a cracker anyway."

"Dat's right, this young cat shoulda kicked his ass."

"No man, how you gon act, that ole man ain't don nothin' but ack like any other white man, sides, he an old fucker."

"Don't make no difference to me, I'da kicked his ole ass."

"You'all missin' the larger point," Rufus said, "I'm old as dat white man and age ain't got nothin' to do wit it. All white people, specially ole ones, gotta be taught they can't keep treatin' us like dogs. Fact is, Negroes been takin' shit from white people for too goddamn long. Far as I'm concerned you did the right thing, son."

"Yeah, guess you right, Rufus," Joe said, "now com'on back to playin' checkers so I can kick yo ass worse'n this young cat woulda kick that white man's ass."

Everyone in the shop laughed at Joe's comment. The tension had passed and the routine of the barbershop returned to normal.

No one had said that maybe I had made a mistake in assuming the old landlord was a racist, and they all ignored the role of the big black woman and her comment on "colored mens." Actually it was a statement they had all probably heard so many times that they were conditioned to ignore it.

As for me, well, I had mixed feelings. Jackson was right, I shouldn't have cursed or threatened the old man. I even felt a little sorry for him and a bit ashamed of myself as I watched the big black woman assisting him. I was immediately touched by her humanity, and years later I strove to understand the significance of her disapproval of "colored mens." Nevertheless, I knew I had done the right thing by not permitting that old white man to treat me like a nigger. On that score my mother and stepfather would have been proud of me.

# CHAPTER 17

# STARLESS NIGHTS

There was a family photo album I enjoyed thumbing through as a child, but it had one snapshot in it that I detested. It was the only photograph of my mother I ever saw in which she looked ugly and absurd. The picture was taken on a camping trip, a short time before her marriage to Lawrence Haynes. In that photo, my mother is wearing a black swimsuit. My future stepfather and two other politely smiling young men are in the foreground while my aunts, Irene and Maudell, stand behind Mother.

Eulalie was uninhibitedly clowning for the camera with a knock-kneed stance. One arm was extended toward the sky while the other hung limply at her side. Her head was cocked to one side, resting on the shoulder of the extended arm; her eyes were crossed and an exaggerated grin completed the distortion of her pretty face. My mother was obviously trying hard to amuse her audience

When I first saw the snapshot as a very young child, I did not recognize the ugly, clowning woman as my pretty mother. It was only after I was repeatedly told it was she that I reluctantly accepted the truth. But I never completely saw that snapshot as the humorous statement my mother obviously intended it to be.

Now, recalling that long ago photograph of Mother, I equate it in my mind with the manic facet of her drinking personality, the altered persona that struck her husband, children and extended family as overbearing, embarrassing and, at times, disgusting.

It is also sadly ironic that when that picture was taken, before Daddy understood the consequences of her drinking, he and Mother occasionally drank together. Little did he know then that he was destined to spend most of the rest of his life trying to get her to stop.

Numerous times when I was a kid Mother got off the sauce for extended periods, once or twice for as long as a year. Whatever the complex of reasons which led her to periodic sobriety, the bottom line was she stopped because she wanted to, and when she reopened the bottle, she was the one who picked the time and place.

Children depend on consistency from the adults closest to them. They feel secure in the knowledge that the loving and dependable Mom and Dad of today will be the same people tomorrow. The child of an alcoholic must live with the reality of a dual personality in the body of a single parent. In my case, I never knew when I'd find the bright, warm, sober mother I loved transformed into the garrulous, maudlin, drunken woman I disliked.

I vividly recall those early drinking days. I would return home from school in the afternoon to find my baby brother, Larry, napping or in his playpen and Mother sitting at the kitchen table talking on the telephone. She would motion me to her with an unusually vigorous wave of her arm, while telling whoever she was talking to that her "darlin' JohnnyBoy was home from schoool."

To me she'd say, "Did you have a possositively wonnurful day, Baby?" Then came the long hug, the kind usually reserved for returning prisoners of war and, finally, the overly wet kiss accompanied by the sickening sweet-sour alcohol smell of her breath.

Sometimes no one would be at home when I returned from school. On those occasions there might be a note informing me that she and little Larry were visiting a friend, or the note would instruct me to retrieve my brother from our grandparents' house and babysit him until she returned home.

Mother and Daddy almost always argued at night following a day when she'd been drinking. Since the rented house we lived in was small, I could easily hear them from my bedroom. If I went to sleep before the argument began, I would invariably be awakened by their loud voices.

My mother and stepfather's arguments were usually fueled by his anger over her drinking and her angry reaction to his criticism of her behavior. Their arguments sometimes descended into the dangerous waters of searing mutual contempt, vicious name-calling and uncontrollable rage and violence.

My parents' arguments frightened me severely when I was a child, often to the point of trembling and tears. My heart would beat wildly from the dread of impending disaster. I would pull the bed covers over my head and curl into a fetal position with my hands tightly pressed against my ears. Paradoxically, I also strained to listen through my own defenses for the reassuring silence, which would mark another truce in the seemingly never ending war between the two people I loved above all others.

There were times when I was five or six years old when I summoned the courage to leave my bed and intervene in an argument that had turned violent. Some external force propelled me into their midst to serve as the embodiment of the message: enough is enough. My small, pajama-clad body would be between the combatants before they realized I was there. Seeing me would startle and, I think, shame them into temporarily halting hostilities. But, occasionally, the fight erupted again after I returned to bed, sometimes more heatedly than before.

I think it's certain that I had a greater impact on my mother's periods of sobriety as a child than I ever had as an adult. Clearly, Mother loved me, and the knowledge that her behavior traumatized me must have caused her considerable pain.

I'm also convinced she believed her drinking was self-destructive and, given her religious leanings, morally wrong. So it was probably her instinct for self- preservation, love of her children and religion, which gave her the strength to periodically stop drinking. Nevertheless, the intractable denial, so common among alcoholics, was characteristic of my mother as well.

Whenever a member of her family challenged her to give up booze, she invariably became defensive and angry. Her typical response to such challenges from me went something like, "I don't have a drinking problem and I resent the suggestion that I do. You mind your own damn business and I'll take care of mine."

She generally delivered statements like this with a steely-eyed intensity, which conveyed an end-of-discussion finality. During my late teen years I occasionally persevered, once or twice even bulldozing my way onto the sensitive terrain of family rejection.

"Well, you may not think you have a problem, but to those of us who love you, it's apparent that you do," I'd once told her. "Mama Peachey and your sisters talk about your drinking all the time. Haven't you noticed how they stay clear of you when you're boozin' it up?"

"How dare you suggest my mother and sisters have ever avoided me," she'd thrown back. "That's a contemptible lie. My family knows what loyalty is all about and rejection has no place in our relationships. Now I'll repeat one last time. I don't have a drinking problem and I'm sick of hearing that you think I do."

Unfortunately, no one in our family had the slightest understanding of alcoholism. I don't believe it occurred to Daddy or to the rest of us that Mother's drinking was symptomatic of deeper psychological issues, which probably needed to be addressed medically. We all thought her sobriety was simply a matter of her deciding not to drink, a decision she often made and sometimes adhered to for many months. So when her promises of abstinence were broken, as they invariably were, I understood those regressions as simple willfulness.

I detested the person my mother became when she drank. As a result, I sided with my stepfather in his opposition to her drinking. As a young child, I became his eyes and ears when he was away from home working to support his family. I kept tabs, as best I could, on her whereabouts, associates and how long she had been drinking. When Daddy returned home from work, I dutifully reported on my mother's alcohol-related activities. The issue for me was simply her drinking. In my child's mind I believed all would be right with the world if only my mother would never drink again, and I hoped my stepfather could help make that happen.

My role as Daddy's ally infuriated Mother. "I'm your mother, you little ingrate. How could you possibly support him against me? You have no idea of the disappointment and pain I've suffered in this marriage. I sacrificed myself to give you a home and you repay me by becoming a nigger Judas -- a despicable little back-stabbing turncoat, that's what you are."

After having recklessly and regrettably dissolved her first marriage, my mother claimed her decision to marry my stepfather was partly a compensatory act taken on my behalf. She had taken us away from a sensitive, loving, devoted father and husband and, in exchange, gave me a caring stepfather and herself a bad marriage. Unfortunately, her sacrifice had unwittingly deprived me as well as herself.

When my mother and stepfather had lovingly forgiven each other following one of their many alcohol related arguments, Mother would invariably turn her wrath on me. In Daddy's presence, she would harangue me for being generally disrespectful toward her; not always responding when she spoke to me, or speaking to her without proper deference. She was careful not to directly excoriate me for assisting Daddy when he was present, but all three of us knew this was the basis of her anger.

I can't remember my stepfather ever coming to my rescue when Mother verbally bashed me for being his ally. His failure to support me was very hurtful and it didn't take me long to realize that Daddy's primary interest was in making and keeping peace with Mother. All else was secondary. I was merely a convenient scapegoat for facilitating the process of their mutual forgiveness and reconciliation. Naturally, I resented how I had been cast and during my adolescence my resentment blossomed into alienation.

My mother worked hard at weakening my alliance with Daddy by telling me that he didn't love me as much as he loved her and my little brother. Once, several hours after she had upbraided me for my open opposition to her drinking, she took my hands in hers and in a voice completely devoid of its previous anger said, "Son, no matter how much you kiss Lawrence's behind, he'll never be your real father. He'll never love you as much as I do and he'll never love you as much as he loves Larry, because Larry is his natural son. Johnny, blood is always thicker than water. So, regardless of what you think of me for occasionally taking a drink, please remember what I have just said to you. It will save you considerable pain in the long run."

I knew there was some truth in my mother's cruel assessment of my place within the Haynes family. Nevertheless, I also knew Daddy needed me and I believed some degree of love was inherent in his need.

Several months before my mother's "blood is thicker than water" statement, Daddy had talked to me about his life insurance policy. He said he was thinking of substituting Little Larry for Mother as the sole beneficiary on the policy and he wanted to know whether I thought it was a good idea.

I remember shrugging my thirteen-year-old shoulders and saying something like, "Yeah, that sounds like the right thing to do," while my heart was breaking because he made no mention of me as a beneficiary. I didn't care in the least about the monetary value of his insurance policy. What I cared about and hungered for intensely was concrete evidence that Daddy loved me as much as he did when I was three years old. The issue for me was not whether he loved me, but rather how much.

I couldn't see the big picture from Daddy's perspective. Here was a hardworking, low-paid man whose assets consisted of a life insurance policy, a drunk for a wife, and two sons, one of whom was a stepson. The stepson had a father and grandparents who were financially able and willing to care for him. But Little Larry's only safety net was his father's whole life policy. Daddy never explained any of this to me, but had he done so it probably wouldn't have helped me to feel as connected to him as I wanted to be.

During my teen years, Mother began to repeatedly hammer home the quicksand-like quality of my position within the Haynes family. She told me how hard she had worked over the years to preserve my image in the minds and hearts of the Martins. I learned for the first time that when my mother and stepfather first married, Daddy had wanted to legally adopt me and Mother had refused to permit it.

She said she refused because she wasn't sure the marriage would last, and those doubts made it doubly important to preserve my connection to my father and his family. She admitted that for a while during her second marriage she had continued to harbor hopes of reuniting with my father. "It wasn't an accident that it took me four years to get pregnant with your stepfather's child," she confessed.

"While my hopes for happiness have long since been dashed, you can still benefit from the Martin relationship. Thanks to me, they've never forgotten you and they love you far more than Mr. Lawrence Haynes is capable of loving you."

What my mother said about her efforts with the Martins over the years was true. She had written regularly to my grandparents and insisted I write to them as well, which I did. My grandparents' letters to me were filled with love and longing for my presence. They sent gifts and money and even bought me the only bicycle I ever owned as a youth. Once, Grandpa Martin visited the Bay Area and came to our Dohr Street house to see me. Several years later Grandma Martin traveled to Oakland to visit a niece, and Mother made sure that I spent time with her.

My mother generally failed to get me to write to my father. Before I entered my teens, I wanted desperately for Daddy to be my only father. The very existence of my real father was a major distraction and tended to confuse and minimize my connection to Lawrence Haynes. My real father and I did not communicate with each other in any meaningful way until I was fourteen.

Mother, on the other hand, continued to carry the torch. It seemed like she telephoned my "real father" every time she had a few drinks. I don't know all of what they talked about. I do know she complained to Dad, as I later called him, about how cruel fate had been to her. That much I occasionally overheard before disgustedly removing myself from hearing range.

Years later, my stepmother, Erma, told me Dad always received Mother's calls and responded to her as empathetically as he could. "John and I were saddened by what Eulalie was doing to herself," Erma said.

When I entered my teens, my mother's periods of sobriety were still identifiable and frequent, but there were changes in her drinking pattern as well. The sober periods were shorter than in earlier years and her drinking episodes were longer, sometimes lasting three or four days. She began to spend more time away from home when she drank and was more neglectful of her family. While Mother had always reacted defensively to criticism of her drinking, the intensity of her denial escalated into an increasingly vitriolic, foul-mouthed scorn of any who dared criticize her.

Meanwhile, my own life was beginning to take unpromising turns, most notable of which was a decidedly average academic performance in junior high school.

My mother had been a constant in my elementary school life, pushing me to excel, helping me with homework, celebrating my accomplishments and maintaining a steady, parental presence at my school.

Suddenly, this changed as I made the transition from a neighborhood elementary school populated by working class children, to a distant junior high attended by kids from Berkeley's wealthiest families. I felt lost in the cool anonymity of junior high and I missed my mother as a parental star in the school environment.

I began to stay out late at night to avoid the home wars between my parents and to enjoy the camaraderie of my sports-minded, nonacademically-oriented friends. My friends and I hung out at a park across the street from my house, or on neighborhood street corners. Sometimes we visited a local pool hall on Adeline Avenue, or aimlessly roamed the streets of South Berkeley. We talked about sports, movies, girls, sex, and the differences between our lives and those of our wealthy white classmates who lived in the Berkeley hills.

One day, while trying to impress my friends, I was caught stealing a cake from a grocery store in downtown Berkeley. Fortunately, the store manager telephoned my mother and she persuaded him to meet with her before reporting the crime to the police. When their meeting ended, the manager had agreed not to report the incident to the police and I went home with Mother.

My mother, with her beauty and charm glittering brightly, convinced the store manager that I did not have a juvenile record, which was true; that I had never before stolen anything, which was not true; and that I was destined to make a major contribution to mankind if the manager refrained from filing a police report, which was a tremendous stretch, even for my mother.

A month or so later I made the mistake of coming home early on the wrong night. There, standing in the living room drunk, was Mother. One look at her told me she was also angry. Daddy was in the kitchen. Whatever had been going on between them was evidently on hold.

"So, Mister High and Mighty, what brings you home so early this evening? Have you run out of grocery stores to rob?"

"C'mon, Mother, you know I've never robbed a store. All I did was take a little cake," I said with a smile, trying to con her out of her hostile state of mind. Then I moved closer to where she stood so I could give her a disingenuous hug. Friendly responses to Mother's drunken attacks sometimes mollified her, sometimes not. The key to being successful was patience, which generally meant taking some of her verbal abuse without reacting angrily. Unfortunately, at fifteen I had too much resentment of my own to carry on a charade with my drunken mother much beyond an initial gesture.

"You deceitful, sneaky, smart ass nigger. You're into something illegal and I know what it is."

Daddy was listening to my mother's baiting attack on me from the sanctuary of the kitchen but, as usual, he said nothing.

"Mother, you don't know a damn thing because I'm not doing anything illegal. I'm with my friends in the evening because I can't stand to be in this house when you're drunk. Why don't you just leave me alone?"

"Don't you raise your voice to me, you ungrateful piece of shit. I won't stand for insolence from you. I almost died giving birth to you and I'm certainly not going to take disrespect from you. Do you understand me, Boy?"

"You started all this senseless crap like you always do when you've been drinking. As far as I'm concerned, you can take your drunken self and go to hell."

I didn't see it coming. The steel reinforced heel of her shoe struck me above my left eyebrow opening a jagged, two-inch cut, which literally spouted blood. Mother continued to babble, but I was too stunned by the blow and the fact that she had hit me to comprehend what she was saying. I remember Daddy telling me to go upstairs and wash the blood from my face. He said he would come up shortly to further examine the wound. I walked slowly to the stairs, and stopped. Mother had entered the kitchen and was standing next to the stove by a large pot of boiling water, staring at me warily. Our eyes met.

Something inside of me snapped. Suddenly, I turned toward the kitchen and moved with catlike quickness toward the woman who had viciously attacked me. All I could see through tear-blurred eyes was a mean drunk who had come within an inch of permanently blinding me in one eye.

I closed in on her as she lifted the pot of boiling water. Daddy, who was washing my blood from his hands, didn't have time to turn from the kitchen sink and intercept me. I don't remember the scalding water ever touching me as it splashed to the floor, but I vividly remember my perfectly thrown overhand right connecting with the hated drunk's face. My assailant fell flat on her back from the force of the punch, and I stepped toward her prone body with more violence in mind. But before I could complete my mission, Daddy's powerful arms encircled my waist and lifted me away from certain tragedy.

I had thrown the right-hand as he had taught me to do years before. I hadn't forgotten his warning about the bad girl that hits you. "My advice to you is to knock her on her ass."

I left the house and walked alone under a starless sky to Herrick Hospital where a sympathetic physician stitched and bandaged my wound.

I spent the night at my friend, Ed Porter's, house. Mrs. Porter told me everything would turn out fine, "because you and your mother love each other." Then she gave me a bowl of tomato soup and a goodnight hug.

I said the Lord's Prayer that night, the way my beautiful mother had taught me to do when I was a small boy. ".... and forgive us our trespasses as we forgive those who trespass against us." I felt a monumental sadness as I drifted off into a fitful sleep.

## CHAPTER 18

# LOVING AFFIRMATION,
# PAIN AND SADNESS

My father and I reconnected in earnest when I was fourteen. I don't know how he knew the time was right, but he did, and it was. He and my stepmother spent twelve hours with me in the Bay Area following his honorable discharge from the Navy in Chicago. Eighteen months later, in 1947, I was living with Dad and Erma and attending school in Houston.

I was, to say the least, initially shocked by the transition from the racially integrated Berkeley High School, with its four square city block campus of solid, well-kept buildings, clean airy classrooms, and groomed athletic fields, to the old, dilapidated single two-storied building which housed the segregated Booker T. Washington High School of Houston, Texas. Amazingly, I not only adapted to that enormous social and environmental change, but I also improved my academic performance from earning C's and B's in Berkeley to A's in Houston.

The Booker T. Washington High I attended, was the same old battered, under funded school for Negro children my mother and father had attended in the 1920s. But the old school was more, much more than a building that probably should have been condemned a decade earlier.

Most of the school's faculty knew my father, and some were his friends. A few had known my mother and remembered her fondly.

"You must be John Martin's son," more than one teacher I had never seen before said while walking past me in a hallway crowded with kids. "Yes, I am." It took me a while to pick up on the sir and ma'am routine. "Well, John, Jr., I'm Mrs. Woods, the geometry teacher. I've known your mother and father forever. They're both wonderful people. We're all glad to have you here, son." And so it went those first few days at Booker T. Washington High School. After a while, some of the faculty began to seem like extended family members. What a dramatic difference it was from the often cool, distant formality of student-teacher relationships I had experienced at Berkeley High.

I took English from Miss Virginia Miller, the strict and impeccably precise grammarian, who had not only taught Mother and Dad, but my five aunts and two uncles as well. Miss Miller remembered them all, but reminisced mainly about my father. "Your father was one of my most brilliant students. Your mother and her sister Louise were pretty good students too, but your father was special. And I expect nothing but the best from you, young man. Nothing but the best."

Mrs. Lillie Richards, my algebra teacher, was a high school classmate and friend of Mother's. "Eulalie and I often walked to school together, and we were always in and out of each other's houses on weekends. I was in her wedding when she married your daddy. I bet you didn't know that, did you?"

"No, uh no ma'am, I didn't."

Mrs. Richards and I instantly liked each other and I looked forward to going to her class. I began to love algebra. I got A's on all the daily homework and on every test. Two years earlier, at Willard Junior High in Berkeley, I had received a D on the same first year algebra curriculum Mrs. Richards taught so adeptly and with a consistently loving nod toward me.

I did struggle in Mr. Henry Greer's physics class. That course was hard. But Mr. Greer was a patient, compassionate teacher and every night my gifted father helped me with the elementary physics problems I found so difficult. It also helped that Dad and Mr. Greer were close friends. More than once I overheard them having a lighthearted telephone conversation about my laborious progress in physics. They also played chess together at our house on weekends, and if I happened to be in view they would both glance at me and Mr. Greer would say "Hi, big guy," and they would both smile mysteriously and return to their game. I knew they were talking about me while playing chess, but I could never catch them at it.

It was surreal having high school teachers who functioned like family. But it was also lovely and unbelievably affirming.

My grandparents, who were still healthy and vigorous, were extremely happy over my return. In fact, all four of the Martins, including Erma who had never had children of her own, functioned as if I had never been away. Suddenly, for the first time in many years, I felt unconditional love and acceptance as part of a healthy family. It all felt so natural, reminiscent of a much earlier period in my young life.

The plan was for me to remain with my father indefinitely and, clearly, that is what I should have done. But my teenage priorities brought me back to Berkeley after only one year in Houston. Daddy wrote that he, Mother and Little Larry missed me terribly and they all wished and hoped I would return home.

Daddy's note triggered memories of good times past, like Christmas mornings. For years, my childhood belief in Santa Claus was lovingly kept alive by the creative machinations of Mother and Daddy. I also remembered Christmas afternoons at Mama and Papa Peachey's house, with the extended family gathered around the tree, opening presents and enjoying an unparalleled collective happiness.

And there were the family auto trips to San Francisco to visit Aunt Bessie, see the sights of the city, eating ice cream cones. Nor could I forget those winter evenings huddled around the radio, listening to episodes of "I Love A Mystery." I cherished that and other memories. It didn't matter to me that those fond experiences had not only been interspersed with madness, terror and pain, but could never be relived.

I sorely missed my Berkeley buddies, as well. It wasn't that I hadn't made new friends in Houston. It was simply that I had known my Berkeley pals longer, and I wanted to be with them again. I was, after all, a teenager.

I also wanted to prove to myself that my outstanding academic performance in the black high school I attended in Houston was no fluke and that I could do equally well in the more competitive environment of predominately white Berkeley.

And last, but not least, there was Houston's pattern of rigid racial segregation. No matter how much I tried to ignore the symbols of the evil system surrounding me, I simply couldn't. I felt a deep sense of humiliation living as a southern Negro. One year was not enough time for me to crawl under the psychological shield of middle-class status, which apparently afforded Negro residents of the South a degree of protective armor against the psychic blows of racial discrimination.

While my Martin family and some other middle class blacks seemed to successfully ignore the racial apartheid of the South, I felt constantly oppressed by it. I did not want to adapt to subservience. I much preferred having the option to kick the shit out of any white boy who crossed me, without fear of being hung from a cottonwood tree.

So I left Houston and my father's loving, emotionally stable home, to return to Berkeley and the unhappy, dysfunctional house of my mother and stepfather.

I found life in the Haynes' household pretty much the same as I had left it, except my forty-year-old mother was pregnant. Several months later my baby sister, Irene, was born. The old specious equation was at work: newborn baby = no more marital problems.

I suspect Daddy thought and, perhaps Mother agreed, that a baby would rejuvenate their marriage, and I'm sure he also believed that the responsibility of caring for a new life would give my mother sufficient incentive to stop drinking. Of course the baby did not correct all or any part of what was wrong in their relationship. While Mother evidently refrained from drinking during pregnancy, and for a short time following Irene's birth, her sobriety did not last.

Soon after I returned to Berkeley, I obtained a part-time job in a local drugstore, which helped to partially distract me from our family problems. I threw myself into my studies and achieved nearly straight A's at Berkeley High during my senior year. When I wasn't working at the drugstore or studying in the public library, I was with my steady girlfriend, Juanita, or hanging out with my best buddies, Ed, Paul, Frank and Le Roy.

I did sleep at home and, for the most part, ate there as well. I slept on a fold down wall bed in the downstairs dining room, while Little Larry and Baby Irene occupied one of the upstairs bedrooms I had previously shared with Larry. The downstairs arrangement was to my liking since it gave me a greater measure of privacy.

*Eulalie in 1952*

However, I also came to realize that as long as I lived with Mother and Daddy, it would be impossible to get away from the drinking and fighting that characterized life in their household.

In August 1950, after completing a year of community college, I left home and moved to Los Angeles where I lived for a short time with my mother's oldest sister, Louise and, later, with a teenaged friend and his mother. Three days after my nineteenth birthday in November, I volunteered for a four-year tour of duty in the United States Air Force.

I was never again a permanent resident in the home of my mother and stepfather, nor was I ever to have a consistent adult friendship with either of them.

In the 1950s my brother Larry took on the child-parent role I had played in earlier years. Larry was stuck in that role at a time when our mother's drinking had long since crossed the line into alcoholism. He and Irene also lacked the loving, nonalcoholic second family refuge, which I had in the Martins.

When I was older, Larry once told me about a few of his childhood experiences with our mother. He was quick to remember with fondness our mother's frequent intercession on his behalf at Longfellow Elementary School in the mid to late 1940s. I smiled as I recalled similar loving experiences. Larry remembered our mother coming to school and introducing herself to every teacher he ever had, then remaining in contact with them throughout the school year.

"At school she was always there for me, Man" he said.

Larry described a time our mother had pleased him tremendously by making cookies for his entire third grade class. That episode triggered his recall of the absolutely delicious lemon meringue pies and chocolate fudge cakes our mother used to make.

We talked on about our mother's good looks and how white people on the street frequently stopped and stared at her when we were with her. We could easily see the unasked question on their faces: "I wonder what a pretty white woman like that is doing with those little darkies?" We laughed long and hard reminiscing on those shared memories.

Larry also recalled how much our mother loved to tease, and when the teasing got to him and he started pouting, she would laugh and hug him until he laughed as well.

"Man, when I was little she used to make me so mad by breaking out in song when it was bedtime. I can still hear her singing "Little Man, You've Had A Busy Day". I hated that fuckin' song. She knew it too. When she saw how pissed I was she'd tickle my ribs and make me laugh in spite of myself."

I told Larry that Mother also sang "Little Man" to me and, sometimes, when she started singin' it I'd start crying, because I didn't want to go to bed. "But, yeah, she never left me sad either. She'd console me with hugs, kisses and laughter."

Larry was reluctant to talk about negative experiences, but I gently persisted, and the mood between us shifted from happy to somber, from loving recollections to remembered pain. When Larry spoke again, his voice was much lower. His speech was deliberate and monotoned, suggesting the pain of the past was not far from the surface; no one ever really lays bad ghosts to permanent rest.

"Shit, Man, I remember so much I'd like to forget but can't," he said so slowly that I thought he might change his mind and say no more. But he continued, "There were so many days I returned home from school to an empty house and she was out there somewhere, drinkin'. And I knew the baby would be with her, 'cause after Mama Peachey moved to Los Angeles to live with Aunt Louise, Mother had no one to leave Irene with when she went out boozin'.

"Instead of goin' out and play, I'd start searching for Mother and Irene. Once, when I was about twelve, I had gone to the houses of several of her drinkin' buddies, but none of 'em had seen her that day. I found myself wandering down Sacramento Street, out of ideas and ready to head back home. I was walking by the Lark's Club and happened to look in the window. I saw Mother sitting at the bar drinkin' with two guys snuggled up on either side of her. One of those assholes had his arm wrapped around her shoulders.

"Man, it's still impossible for me to put the right words on the pain, shame, and fear I felt seeing Mother like that. I wanted to run away, far away and do something to erase that image from my mind. But I didn't run away, 'cause Irene was in her stroller at Mother's feet. Her little mouth was puckered up like she had just finished cryin', or was getting ready to cry, I don't know.

"Anyway, I just walked into the fuckin' bar, grabbed the handle of the stroller and told Mother I was taking Irene home. I remember pleading with Mother to come home with us. But she said, 'No, go on, get outta here.' God, I can still feel my mouth trembling and the hot tears in my eyes as I pushed Irene's stroller outta that stinkin' bar on our way home without Mother. Hours later Daddy dragged Mother outta the Larks Club."

When Larry finished talking, we both sat very still, silently reflecting on the unhappiness of the past. The story triggered a raft of unpleasant memories for both of us. I didn't ask him to share another.

Mother went through a short period of sustained sobriety following Mama Peachey's death on November 30, 1961, at age eighty-five. My mother seemed to be spending considerable time in sober reflection on facets of Mama's life. She wrote to me as I was preparing to leave Medford, Massachusetts, after deciding to discontinue advanced graduate study at Tufts University.

*Dear Johnny:*

*I was saddened to learn you had decided to end your pursuit of a doctoral degree in sociology, but then I realized you must do what you think is best for your family. I can understand how difficult it* must be to work as a resident advisor for freshmen, while living in their dormitory with your wife and three-year-old son. At least you have your Master's degree and prospects for a bright future. I'm very proud of you, as I've always been.

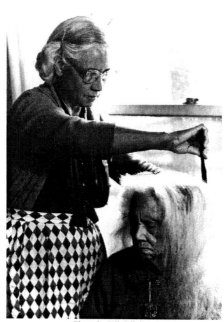
Photo by Bill Gillohm.
*Eldest daughter, Louise, combing Mama Peachey's hair in the early 1960's.*

The memory of my dear, departed mother is never far from my mind these days. She was such an angel of a human being, a woman whose entire life was one of loving sacrifice for others. You know, Son, I firmly believe it was Mama's unbending faith in God that gave her the strength to successfully live the life she lived.

Can you imagine the shock of learning you're a Negro in this racist country after living as a white person for the first fifteen or sixteen years of your life? In some parts of the world it wouldn't have made any difference, but, honey, we're talking about the American South in the late 19th century. The drastic change that transformation caused in the life of her father, your great-grandfather, led to his early death. But Mama not only survived, she did so with grace and dignity. She even learned to lovingly embrace being colored, up to a point (smiles).

For all of her adult life with Papa, she lived in poverty, and that didn't dampen her spirits either. Neither did she seem to resent caring for Papa when he got older, even after he started drinking too much and became withdrawn and sullen in his last years.

She gave birth to nine babies over a sixteen-year span and with each birth she experienced a new sense of exaltation. She even seemed to gain renewed strength from giving birth. Hell, my depression was so great after your birth I almost went totally nuts. She was an amazing woman, Johnny.

Did you realize that preparing food for her family was a spiritual experience for Mama? Well, it was. It was as if God enveloped her heart and hands as she prepared and cooked

sumptuously healthy meals for those she loved. I'm not sure there was anything in life she enjoyed doing more than preparing food for her family. But, then, her family was her life.

A few years before her large heart failed, she was completely blind from glaucoma, and could

Eulalie with grandson Michael Martin,
June 1958

barely hear or care for herself. Yet the sweetness of her disposition never changed. Mama was a Saint, Johnny, sent to live among us mortals so we could see God's Way by HOW she lived her life. And show us she did. Even if we never lived up to her high standards, through her we were able to see how strength and courage and goodness can actually flourish in the face of adversity.

175

*I only wish for the sake of my children that I could have been*
*a replica of my dear mother. But, alas, as you well know, that did*
*not come to pass. However, I do believe, as Mama taught me and*
*I tried to teach you, that in spite of our weaknesses and failings an*
*abiding faith in God will pull us through in the long run.*

*Give my love to Jasmine and my beautiful little grandson,*
*Michael.*

*I hope to see all of you soon.*

*I remain, as always,*

*Your Loving Mother, Eulalie.*

I too loved and adored my grandmother, and I would miss her. She had lived a remarkable life as a white-black woman in race conscious America, and I believed that the racial implications of her life would impact her descendants for generations.

In 1963, Jasmine and I were back in Berkeley, living on College Avenue and expecting our second child, when I received a telephone call from my mother. She was calling from Highland Hospital in Oakland, where she had just been released following a four day stay. She had been admitted to the hospital for observation after my brother and I found her unconscious in a neighbor's home. She had been drinking for three days straight. Although Mother had been hospitalized at Highland several times, the circumstances surrounding her other visits had a slightly different twist.

At least twice that I recall during the mid to late 1940s, Daddy had attempted to have Mother committed to a state mental hospital to cure her of her drinking. Highland's psychiatric ward had been the first stop in the involuntary commitment process.

I don't believe he ever really understood or accepted his inability to control my mother's drinking, despite his long and ardent efforts. I think, with my stepfather, the issue (at least at some level) was reduced to a contest of wills. He saw it as his will against hers. Since no one in the family understood alcoholism as an illness, the rationale for psychiatric commitment was not treatment but punishment.

On those occasions when my stepfather succeeded in getting my mother admitted for observation to the psychiatric ward at Highland Hospital, she was generally too drunk to realize what was happening to her. He would return home hopeful that his wife would eventually rejoin him as a new woman after having been subdued into sobriety. Unfortunately, from Daddy's perspective, observation was merely the first step in the involuntary commitment procedure. The process also included a formal legal hearing.

The observation period was long enough for my mother to detox and to begin to feel physically fit. Canny fox that she was, she would soon begin assisting overworked staff in ministering to the needs of other patients, which naturally endeared her to those assigned to observe her. At no time during those brief hospital stays did Mother exhibit behavior which the Highland staff assessed as mental illness warranting involuntary commitment to a state mental institution.

Daddy would stand before the hearing panel and describe the radical change in his wife's personality when she was under the influence of alcohol, as well as her failure to stop drinking despite repeated attempts to do so over the years. As it invariably happened, the bizarre behavior Daddy described was not at all consistent with how Mother had conducted herself while under observation by hospital staff.

My mother would deny all of her husband's allegations, including consistent heavy drinking, with just the right amount of righteous indignation. She suggested that perhaps it was he and not she who should be committed. The outcome was always the same. The panel would decide there was no evidence of mental disorder which justified institutionalization, and Lawrence and Eulalie Haynes would go home and resume their dysfunctional lives together.

When Mother telephoned me from Highland Hospital that day in 1963, I heard a soft, sad, slightly quavering voice asking me to drive to the hospital and take her home. I'll never forget how pale she was. There were beads of perspiration forming a line above her upper lip and dotting her nose. Her hands trembled uncontrollably. As we drove, she talked of ending her tumultuous twenty-eight year marriage to Lawrence Haynes. Jasmine, always empathetic and generous, joined me in inviting my mother to stay with us until she decided if a divorce was what she really wanted. If she ended her marriage, where would she live and how would she support herself? These were questions she had to address and perhaps being separated from her husband for a time would help her to think more clearly.

My mother lived with us for about two weeks, mostly confining herself to the dining room couch where she also slept. She would still be asleep every morning when I left for work. And when I returned in the evening, she would usually be sitting stoically on the couch with a blank look on her face and a wan smile of greeting. I learned from Jasmine, who never once complained about Eulalie's presence in our home, that Mother took brief solitary walks, helped around the house, but also appeared to be quite sad.

Mother and Daddy arranged to see each other after she had been with us for several days. Daddy parked his car on the street in front of our house and Mother went out to meet with him. They had been outside sitting in the car for about an hour when I decided to check on them.

I approached the car, but remained a discreet distance behind it. I saw them clearly through the rear window of the car. They sat on opposite ends of the front seat, both looking straight ahead, both immobile. It was the last time I ever saw them together.

How strange that my final images of my mother together with each of her two husbands, twenty-four years and two thousand miles apart, was in the front seats of automobiles. And in both instances I was a silent witness, viewing the scenes from behind the actors.

One evening after my mother left our house, I found over a dozen empty wine and whiskey bottles underneath the couch she slept on during her stay with us. She must have forgotten they were there, because she could have easily disposed of them in an outside public trash bin and we never would have known. I later learned from the manager of the grocery store across from our house that she had made daily purchases of wine or whiskey. I gave up on my mother after discovering those bottles. I believed then that Mother and alcohol were permanently linked, and I neither wanted a drunk in my life nor to impose one on my growing family.

Not long after her stay with us ended, Mother and Daddy divorced and went their separate ways. Daddy married Onita Crawford, the lady he had been engaged to when Mother and I arrived in Berkeley in 1933. Irene, who was then a teenager, lived with them until she finished high school and went to work for the Pacific Gas and Electric Company in Oakland.

It was I who pulled away from Daddy during my late adolescence. Years earlier I had come to believe that I did not have his unqualified love as a son, and that our only positive connection was as allies in our opposition to Mother's drinking. I had been deeply hurt by his failure to come to my aid when my mother heaped scorn and abuse upon me for being his ally.

Although I was nearing forty-five when he died in 1976, Daddy and I never discussed the reasons for our estrangement. I was so caught up in my growing family and career that I had no interest in dealing with past emotional issues.

*Maria Martin*

During Daddy's final illness I visited him in the hospital as often as I could. One day I talked to him about how well my brother, Larry, was doing in his new career as a radio newscaster. "Daddy, you must be very proud of your son." He smiled, nodded agreement, gripped my arm and as our eyes met he said, "I'm very proud of both of my sons." Those were the last words I can remember him saying to me. I cried uncontrollably after leaving the hospital that day.

Years after his brief career as a radio newscaster, my brother Larry would become a very successful entrepreneur. He owned and sold radio stations, a commercial bank and several other businesses. He married three times, but neither he nor our sister Irene ever had children.

*Michael Martin*                    *Charles Martin*

In the mid-1960s I went to work in President Lyndon Johnson's Anti-Poverty Program in San Francisco, first as an Area Coordinator with the Community Action Program and then as the Social Services Advisor for the federal Model Cities project. Jasmine and I purchased our first home on Deakin Street in Berkeley, where we lived for four years before moving with our three children, Michael, Charlie and Maria, to Marin County in 1968.

In 1980, after twenty-eight years of marriage, I left Jasmine for a younger woman. Her name was Sierra. She was white, vulnerable, very pretty and quickly pregnant by me. She was twenty-one years my junior, and she was also a heroically recovering alcoholic. We married on the anniversary of my father's birthday, November 21, 1981, a day after my divorce from Jasmine was finalized.

Seventeen years later, Sierra suddenly left me to reestablish a relationship with an enormously patient suitor whom she had refused to marry two and a half decades earlier. The pain of losing Sierra and our beautiful sixteen-year-old daughter, Alexis, was excruciating. My entire adult life, all forty-six years of it, had revolved around two wives and four children, and I had dearly loved them all. Then at sixty-seven years of age the only life and happiness I had known as an adult suddenly, crushingly ended, and I was alone. In the midst of my devastation I recalled a lesson Mother occasionally repeated when I was a child, "Always remember, Son, the pain you cause others is likely to visit you in the future. What goes around comes around." At that moment I remembered dear Jasmine, and the hurt I had visited upon her when I left her for a younger woman.

And Mother? In 1963, for the first time in her life, she was completely isolated from family. Mama, Papa and Tom, Jr. had died. She was divorced from her second husband, alienated from her three children and shunned by her remaining brother and five sisters. Fortunately, charitable people without lifelong connections to my mother came to her aid during that dark period of her life when she needed support and assistance the most.

Reverend Jones, the minister of the Oakland African Methodist Episcopal Church where Mother regularly attended, helped her to obtain lodging at the Good Samaritan Home in Oakland. Church members comforted her with their visits and dinner invitations. A sympathetic county welfare worker facilitated the processing of an application for indigent care and later helped my mother obtain temporary work and more permanent lodging. After leaving the short-term shelter of the Good Samaritan Home, Mother was able to rent a comfortable room in the home of an elderly couple on 11th Avenue in Oakland. Later, she moved into an apartment of her own on Ashby Avenue in Southwest Berkeley.

I made no effort to see my mother as she, with the help of loving and generous black and white people I did not know, put the pieces of her life back together. I can only guess that she must have been periodically sober as she bravely confronted the daunting task of establishing a new life at age fifty-six, without money, shelter, a job, or family support of any kind.

I'll never know for certain, but I can't shake the feeling that my mother's possible recovery from alcoholism may have been at its highest potential for success during that time she courageously faced the total restructuring of her life. She had evidently hit rock bottom and then apparently climbed out of the pit to achieve a measure of self-sufficiency. If she had had the love and support of family at that time, it might have helped her achieve a lasting sobriety.

It was years after her death, when alcoholism was generally defined as a disease and recovery programs had become commonplace, that I began to understand the nature of my mother's illness. It was then that I often fantasized myself as a less self-absorbed son, financing a twenty-eight day stay for Mother at a recovery center for alcoholics. Then helping her attend AA meetings. Those fantasized AA meetings always included at least a few college-educated mulatto women with backgrounds similar to my mother's --- women who had histories of divorce and who had suffered alienation from their families.

In my fantasy my mother bonded with those recovering women as closely and lovingly as she had with her sisters in another life. The fantasy ends with Mother becoming strong in recovery and living a healthy life filled with travel, good friends and an adoring, loving family.

In reality, that optimal time for intervention had passed when I grudgingly began receiving Mother's final drink-and-dial telephone calls -- about eighteen months before the Alameda County Coroner awakened me at 3:10 a.m. on that rainy December morning in 1969.

## CHAPTER 19

# THE *ONE-DROP RULE*
# IN TRANSITION

It has been over thirty-five years since my mother was struck down by a school van on a rain-drenched street in Berkeley, California. My memory of the Alameda County Coroner informing me by telephone of her death remains quite vivid. So, too, does his epithetic categorization of her dead body as that of a negress.

What I found even more disturbing than the offensive racial label, was the inadequate racial classification given to my mother in life and in death. Genetically, my mother was more white than black. Yet, in racist America, she had no other honorable choice than to live her life as a black woman. She was a classic victim of America's *One-drop Rule*, an enduring racist policy first invoked to create more slaves, and then accepted for over three centuries by both whites and blacks.

The *One-drop Rule* has encouraged racism among whites through its implicit denial of the biological connection between whites and blacks through their common mulatto link, thereby fostering the absurd notion of racial purity. Blacks for their part shrugged and shrewdly galvanized around the *One-drop Rule* to create a powerful beige-tan-brown-black phalanx, with the eradication of racial discrimination as its single-minded mission. And, in the beginning, that was a good thing.

Unfortunately, the perpetuation of a lie, for whatever reason, can and does create casualties. Thus, the complicity of whites and blacks in upholding the standard of the *One-drop Rule* denied millions of people of partial African descent the ability to openly identify with the totality of their ancestry and be recognized as multiracial by society.

In the mid-1960s I once shared a flight from Washington, D.C. to San Francisco with two friends. Both were white, highly educated and possessed firm commitments to the elimination of racial injustice in the United States. At one point during the trip our conversation turned to a lighthearted discussion of respective backgrounds.

Both of my friends laughingly referred to themselves as mongrels, while listing the various European ethnicities which comprised their ancestries. I then joined in the spirit of the moment and told my friends of my African, English, French, Seminole Indian pedigrees. When I finished, there was no response from either man.

Those two sensitive souls were deeply embarrassed for me. They had assumed I could not possibly have English, French and Seminole Indian ancestry. They believed I had fabricated these ancestral connections in order to contribute to the conversation and, sadly, to convince myself, and others, that I was not exclusively black. It had been a light, uncomplicated conversation among friends until it suddenly became contaminated with the legacy of the *One-drop Rule*.

This bogus Americanism is so powerful and pervasive that it has throttled public recognition of the multiracial identities of people with African genes for almost four centuries. Today there are broad-based public rumblings of discontent over the way America racially classifies its citizens. The nucleus of this opposition comes from people in interracial marriages, and from their children. The number of interracial couples in the United States rose by 535 percent between 1960 and 1980 to nearly 2 percent of all married couples. By 1990 it had risen to 2.7 percent.[17] While blacks are still less likely than other races to marry outside their group, they too are contributing to this dramatic upsurge in interracial marriages.

In 1986, over 10% of black men who married outside of the South married white women, up from 3.9% in 1968. The respective rates for black women marrying white men outside of the South were 3.7% and 1.2%. In the South, the rate for black men jumped from 0.24% to 4.2%.[18]

It is the mixed-race children, the offspring of today's interracial couples, who are likely to be the ultimate catalysts in ending the *One-drop Rule*. According to a 1994 article in the New Yorker Magazine, "The number of children living in families where one parent is white and the other is black, Asian, or American Indian has tripled -- from fewer than four hundred thousand in 1970 to one and a half million in 1990 -- and this doesn't count the children of single parents or children whose parents are divorced."[19]

Social analysts at both ends of the American ideological spectrum seem to agree on the potential impact of interracial marriage and the mixed-race children these unions produce. Douglas Besharov of the conservative American Enterprise Institute suggests that the complex racial identity of mixed-race children may be "the best hope for the future of American race relations."[20] Communitarian Sociologist Amitai Etzioni of American University argues that letting people define themselves as multiracial "has the potential to soften the racial lines that now divide America by rendering them less like harsh, almost immutable, caste lines."[21]

---

[17] Todd Gitlin, *The Twilight of Common Dreams* (New York: Henry Holt, 1995), 108.
[18] Ibid, 109.
[19] Lawrence Wright, "One Drop of Blood," *The New Yorker Magazine*, July 25, 1994, p.49.
[20] Jack E. White, "I'm Just Who I am," *Time Magazine*, May 5, 1997, p. 33.
[21] Ibid, 33-34.

Today, American golf sensation Tiger Woods can steadfastly refuse to publicly identify as exclusively African American. His racial heritage is African, Asian, Caucasian and American Indian. As a child, Mr. Woods created the term Cablinasian, to describe his racial heritage. And during an April 22, 1997 interview on "The Oprah Winfrey Show;" he openly discussed his multiracial background; a public discourse carefully avoided by mixed-race African Americans of earlier generations.

To learn that someone could be both African American and multiracial probably confused the hell out of most whites watching Oprah that day. Blacks weren't at all surprised. In fact, Mr. Woods' embracing his multiracial heritage resulted in many blacks publicly denouncing him for "abandoning the race." I suspect many other blacks secretly applauded Woods for publicly saying what they had always wanted to say about themselves, but feared negative social repercussions from doing so.

Tiger Woods, while something of an anomaly among blacks for speaking out publicly on this issue, is not alone in having strong feelings regarding his true racial heritage. There are probably thousands upon thousands of similar examples likely to be found among less celebrated African Americans throughout the country.

In 1990, a white woman married to a black man in Georgia received a census form and saw that it did not have a racial box for her multiracial children.[22] She was outraged. But, unlike white-black women of an earlier era who also had multiracial children, she refused to check the box for black as required by the *One-drop Rule*. Instead, she contacted the Census Bureau, voiced her objection to the form's limitations and pushed for the inclusion of a multiracial classification.

In 1995, another white woman, whose husband was of African and Native American descent, engaged the American Civil Liberties Union to help force her son's Florida public school to increase its racial options on

---

[22] Lawrence Wright, 17.

school registration forms. After much debate, the school agreed to add a multiracial box. However, the parents remained dissatisfied because the tri-racial option they wanted was still denied.[23]

In both of these examples, it was not the black partner who initiated the fight for multiracial recognition -- and that may reveal a great deal about American race history. American blacks have been multiracial for at least three and half centuries and, for just as long, the bulk of white

society has adamantly refused to acknowledge this reality. This is what the *One-drop Rule* is all about. In the face of centuries of conditioning in which black people have seen their own white blood relatives defined as black, it is of little wonder that blacks may not be aggressive participants in the new multiracial advocacy sweeping the nation.

*Alexis Martin, 3 years, 5 months*

On the other hand, any white person who goes into a multiracial union enters the arena wearing the lifelong privilege of his or her whiteness. Many may be determined not to give up the psychological advantages inherent in their racial birthright; it probably follows that if enough whites become personally involved in the multiracial equation, the issue will finally be pushed to the forefront of the American conscience.

The year 2000 census became a focus for mixed-race people seeking to expand America's racial identification options. They lobbied strongly for the addition of a multiracial category and a spirited national debate

---

[23] Jack E. White, 33.

resulted. Ironically, much of the opposition to the just cause of multiracial people came from the civil rights establishment.

The opposition from blacks stems from a conviction that a multiracial census box will lead to a diminution of the national effort necessary to address the real problems of poor blacks. The concern is that "blacks" of more obvious mixed genealogies will correctly identify themselves as multiracial if given

*John Martin w/daughter Alexis*

the opportunity to do so, thus reducing the number of blacks in the population and eroding the group's influence.

Advocates for Asians also share this concern since several of the subgroups currently identified as Asian have very high percentages of interracial marriage. For example, 65 percent of Japanese Americans are marrying outside of their race.[24]

The Census Bureau, after considerable political debate, decided that people responding to the 2000 census would be permitted to identify themselves as members of more than one racial group.

Be this as it may, the truth is that the ultimate fate of the *One-drop Rule* will not to be determined by Census Bureau decisions. It is more likely that parents of mixed-race children and multiracial people

---

[24] Todd Gitlin, 109.

themselves will be the defining force; the demise of the *One-drop Rule* in relation to mixed-race blacks will simply be a byproduct of a growing societal acceptance and embracing of its multiracial reality.

There is, to be sure, a numbing irony about the projected new era. As I look at the cover of the special Fall 1993 issue of Time magazine, I see the face of an absolutely beautiful young woman. She is a computerized creation from a racial mix of Anglo-Saxon, Middle Eastern, African, Asian, Southern European and Hispanic prototypes.

The caption on the cover reads, "The New Face of America." Under the main caption in smaller print is, "How Immigrants Are Shaping the World's First Multicultural Society."[25] The irony is that the lovely face touted as a future ideal has striking similarities to the faces of black-white women, including my grandmother and her daughters, and their daughters and granddaughters, who have been part of the American racial landscape for four hundred years.

But there is hope. Within this social context emerged the magnetic mulatto presence of Barack Obama and his electrifying keynote address to the 2004 Democratic National Convention in Boston. Obama, the forty-two-year old son of a black African father and a white American mother, reminded the national television audience that we are, in essence, One America, a nation undivided by our racial, regional and political differences. His considerable oratorical brilliance aside, Mr. Obama may have stood on that podium before his vast audience as another embodiment of the beginning of the end of the *One-drop Rule*.

Standing tall before his fellow countrymen, with the infusion of his black and white blood lines emanating from his café au lait colored face, Mr. Obama embraced his multiracial background while exhorting his fellow citizens to live up to our creed of one nation indivisible. And, by most fair-minded accounts, millions upon millions of Americans who

---

[25] *Time Magazine*, Special Issue, Fall, 1993, cover page

heard Barack Obama's speech that night in the city where the struggle for our nation's freedom was born, embraced both the man and his message; strong evidence that final rites for the *One-drop Rule* are in the process of being written.

*Alexis at 15 years of age*

Through eyes the color of tropical blue-green-gray oceans, my twenty-two year old daughter, Alexis, who is African American, and Native American, and English, and Irish, and French, and Spanish, and Lebanese, surveys and embraces a multiracial, multicultural world of close friends, suitors, and life experiences, which her grandmother, Eulalie, almost never encountered, even in her dreams.

I am certain my mother would cry prideful tears of joy if she could witness the multiracial lives of all of her grandchildren and great-grandchildren and their children to come, representing the ultimate elimination of the *One-drop Rule*, forever.

# JOHN A. MARTIN, JR

John Martin was raised from a toddler to a young adulthood in Berkeley, California, where he later spent the bulk of his professional career, as the general director of a social service agency. His life journey has included four years of service in the U.S. Air Force, B.A. and M.A. degrees from San Francisco State University and the University of Omaha respectively, post Master's degree study at Tufts University and the University of California at Berkeley, and a wonderfully satisfying professional life working in anti-poverty programs, social service, education, and civil rights organizations. He is a former Chair of the California State Fair Employment and Housing Commission, and the 1996 recipient of the prestigious Benjamin Ide Wheeler Award for Distinguished Community Service. John is the father of four children, and the grandfather of four.

John Martin's interest in American race relations is so deeply embedded in his family heritage, that he finds it impossible to identify its beginnings. He believes that race as a social construct became an unavoidable fact of life at the point of conception for most African Americans of his generation. Nevertheless he considers himself fortunate to be a small part of the continuing movement toward a brother/sisterhood in America, which transcends race. John Martin fervently hopes that *When White Is Black*, his first published book, will offer some help in our ongoing quest to understand and move beyond the many onerous repercussions of race in America.